# COCK ROBIN

# COCK ROBIN

### *A Play in Three Acts*

BY

ELMER RICE

AND

PHILIP BARRY

## SAMUEL FRENCH

Thos. R. Edwards   Managing Director

NEW YORK      LOS ANGELES

SAMUEL FRENCH Ltd.   LONDON

1929

MANUFACTURED IN THE UNITED STATES OF AMERICA
BY THE VAIL-BALLOU PRESS, INC., BINGHAMTON, N. Y.

"COCK ROBIN" was first produced by Guthrie McClintic on January 12, 1928 at the Forty-Eighth Street Theatre in New York City. The play was directed by Mr. McClintic, the settings were designed by Jo Mielziner, and the cast was as follows:

GEORGE McAULIFFE............................*Edward Ellis*
JULIAN CLEVELAND................*Moffat Johnston*
RICHARD LANE...................*Richard Stevenson*
HANCOCK ROBINSON............*Harry D. Southard*
JOHN JESSUP........................*James Todd*
ALICE MONTGOMERY.................*Beatrice Herford*
CARLOTTA MAXWELL.................*Muriel Kirkland*
CLARKE TORRANCE................*Howard Freeman*
HENRY BRIGGS........................*Jo Milward*
DOCTOR EDGAR GRACE..............*Wright Kramer*
MARIA SCOTT.....................*Beulah Bondi*
HELEN MAXWELL.................*Desmond Kelley*

## ACTION AND SCENE

The action of the Play takes place between
four o'clock and ten o'clock, P. M.,
of a single day.

The Scene represents the stage setting of a
group of Amateur players, the interior
of an English grog-shop of the
Eighteenth Century.

### ACT I
The Setting viewed from the front of the Theatre.

### ACT II
The Setting viewed from the rear of the Stage,
looking toward the back of the Front
Curtain, and the Audience.

### ACT III
The same as Act II.

# ACT ONE

# ACT ONE

*Scene: The stage-setting of a group of amateur players, representing the interior of an English grog-shop of the Eighteenth Century, as seen from the front of the theatre.*

*It is a large square room, with dingy plastered walls, dark wood beams and wainscoating, and a beamed ceiling. It is below the street level, and the outside light comes in only through two high, small oblong windows, one in the back wall up Left and one in the Left side wall above the stairs leading upwards to the street door. In the Right side wall up Right is a small doorway on a low platform reached by a couple of steps, the door leading to one of the other rooms of the place. Midway of the Back wall is a large fireplace and mantel dark with smoke and age, and with two or three pewter jars on the mantel. Along the Left side wall a short flight of steps with a rough wooden balustrade leads upwards from a low platform up Left to a six-foot high platform down Left on which is a door opening inwards and leading to the street outside. Against the side wall, Right, stands a large old Dutch sideboard, used as a back bar, and dressed with pewter and earthen mugs, plates, wine bottles, etc. Down Right below this sideboard stands an empty wine barrel on which is an old copper oil container, and still below this stands a straight chair. On the Right side wall in extreme upper corner, is a set of two small shelves six feet from the floor, on which is an*

3

*earthen jar arranged with a trick trigger to be broken,
and a small pewter pot. On the back wall up Right is a
row of wooden clothes pegs, upon which hang three
cloaks. On the Back wall at up Left, below the high win-
dow is a rack in which are a number of long clay church-
warden pipes. At down Right standing in front of the
sideboard is a long tavern table to act as a serving bar,
on which are two small wine casks with taps. At down
Right Center just to left of above table are two square
wooden tavern stools. At up Right Center is a round
topped tavern table upon which are several mugs, with
a straight tavern chair at either side of it, and a square
stool behind it. At up Left Center is a small hexagon
topped table on which is also a mug, and with a straight
chair at Right of, and another one behind it, also a stool
at Left of it. Standing up and down at Left against
the parallels supporting the steps and platform is
another long tavern table. At Right Center and at Left
Center are two large wrought-iron framed, hexagon
shaped hanging lanterns with grimy, dingy glass panels,
each hanging by a single chain.*

*Time: The time is about five in the afternoon, at the
final or dress rehearsal of the amateur player group,
before the performance to be given the same evening.*

*At Rise: The scene is lighted by the dull light of the
two hanging lanterns, while outside the doors Right
and Left as opened the entrances are seen to be dimly
lighted. The blue light of the night outside shows
through the opaque windows at back Left, and at Left.
There are discovered:* HANCOCK ROBINSON, RICHARD
LANE, HELEN MAXWELL, JULIAN CLEVELAND, DR. EDGAR
GRACE, ALICE MONTGOMERY, JOHN JESSUP *and* CARLOTTA
MAXWELL. LANE *is standing at Center his arms folded*

*across his chest, the others, with the exception of* CAR-
LOTTA *and* ROBINSON, *are gathered about him whispering audibly among themselves.* CARLOTTA *sits a little
apart on a stool, her head buried in her arms across a
table.* ROBINSON *stands with one elbow on the bar trying
to appear at ease. He eyes the others narrowly, and
fingers the hilt of his sword with a gloved hand. There
is a general air of expectancy. A moment after the Curtain rises,* GEORGE MCAULIFFE *enters from the door near
the bar up Left, with a brace of long-barrelled pistols
in each hand. As he comes down Right behind the bar
and deposits the pistols upon it, all the others move a
little in that direction excepting* CARLOTTA *and* LANE,
*who do not change their positions.*

MCAULIFFE (*with a grin as he leans his forearms on the
bar*)

There, my fighting cocks—I give my guests what they
demand! Pistols be out of season now, but here you
have 'em!

CLEVELAND (*pulling* LANE *by the arm*)

Come, Jemmy—praying won't steady thy hand any.

LANE (*wrenching his arm free*)

Praying? Me? *He's* the one who needs prayers.
[*He strides over to the bar next to* ROBINSON. *The
others form a tense group about them.*

ROBINSON (*to* LANE)

Will you choose?

LANE (*with a mocking bow*)

After you, m'lord.

ROBINSON (*angrily*)

I'm a commoner like yourself, do you understand?

LANE (*as before*)

Yes, m'lord—or more so.

[*There is a titter of laughter from the* OTHERS. ROBINSON *is about to make an angry retort, then turns to the pistols, examining and weighing them in his hand, until he finally decides upon one.*

ROBINSON (*as he turns away with the pistol*)

This will do me.

LANE (*as he selects one of the remaining pistols*)

So will this.

[*There is suppressed laughter and excited murmurings among the* OTHERS.

Spread out, you—give us a little elbow-room.

[*The* OTHERS *edge away.* GRACE, MRS. MONTGOMERY, *and* JESSUP, *turn to the tables at the rear and take positions near* CARLOTTA. CLEVELAND *and* MRS. MAXWELL *remain downstage at end of bar.*

CLEVELAND

It is agreed between you—six paces, turn and fire?

LANE

Agreed!

[*He strides to the middle of the stage.*

ROBINSON (*contents himself with a nod. He takes off his gloves, throws them on the floor, and fumbling in his pocket produces a gold coin and throws it on the bar*)

To pay for your broken crockery, landlord.

JESSUP (*mockingly, before* MCAULIFFE *can reply*)

There'll be naught broke, save your wishbone maybe.

[*There is jeering laughter from the others, while* MCAULIFFE *pockets the coin and grins.* ROBINSON *goes to Center of the stage.*

JESSUP (*nudges* CARLOTTA *as* ROBINSON *moves*)

Don't 'e want to see him let the air into thy sweetheart?

MRS. MONTGOMERY (*slapping* JESSUP *across the mouth*)

Leave the girl be!

[JESSUP *retreats angrily towards Left.* CARLOTTA *has not moved.*

[ROBINSON *and* LANE *take up their positions at Center back to back,* LANE *facing downstage Left and* ROBINSON *upstage Right.*

CLEVELAND (*his arm about* MRS. MAXWELL'S *waist*)

Are you ready?

LANE

Ready as rain.

ROBINSON

I am ready.

⎫
⎬ (together)
⎭

[*Suddenly just as* CLEVELAND *is about to begin to count,* CARLOTTA *springs to her feet, rushes to* LANE, *and throws herself upon him.*

CARLOTTA (*hysterically*)

I beg thee—beg thee!

LANE (*flinging her roughly aside*)

Get off, thou slut! Thou bag of—who'll pluck this leech off me?

[GRACE *and* JESSUP *raise her to her feet and pull her back to the rear of the room.*

ROBINSON (*over his shoulder to* CARLOTTA)

Have no fear for me, pretty chick.

CLEVELAND

Are you ready?

LANE

Since yesterday, thick-skull.

ROBINSON

Give us the count.

[*The two men are standing back to back as before. At the Rear* DR. GRACE *and* JESSUP *are holding the hysterical* CARLOTTA. MRS. MONTGOMERY *is also at the Rear.*

[MCAULIFFE *is crouched behind the bar well downstage, in Front of the bar are* CLEVELAND *and* MRS. MAXWELL.

CLEVELAND (*counting slowly*)

One—Two—Three—Four—Five—Six!

[*With each count* LANE *and* ROBINSON *take one step forward, till at the end of the sixth step* LANE *is well in corner Down Left, and* ROBINSON *is well in corner Up Right. Simultaneously they turn, take aim, and fire. Only one shot is heard, however.*

ROBINSON (*dropping his pistol*)

God! It caught me! I'm—I'm—

[*He staggers forward three or four paces to Center.*

CARLOTTA (*wrenching herself free*)

Harry! Harry!

[*She rushes forward followed by* GRACE *and* MRS. MONTGOMERY, *as* CLEVELAND *and* MRS. MAXWELL *rush*

*Up from their positions Down Right. They all reach* ROBINSON *as he stops and sways for a moment, and as he starts to fall back insensible, they gradually lower him to the floor, where he lies motionless.* CARLOTTA *flings herself upon him.* GRACE *and* MRS. MAXWELL *pull her away as* CLEVELAND *stoops over the body. While this is in progress* MCAULIFFE *has been leaning curiously across the bar, and on the other side of the stage* JESSUP *and* LANE *have been whispering inaudibly and looking in the direction of the entrance door at the top of the steps Left.*

CLEVELAND (*looking up*)

Clean through, east to west. He breathes, though.
[*At this instant the entrance door at top of the steps Down Left is flung violently open and* CLARKE TORRENCE *appears at the head of the steps. He hesitates a moment then cries as he rushes down the steps.*

TORRENCE

The Guard! The Guard! Did'st hear that volley? Jemmy! For thy life!
[*As he finishes the words he falls headlong.* JESSUP *and* LANE *run over to him, and are joined by* CLEVELAND, DR. GRACE, MRS. MAXWELL, *and* MRS. MONTGOMERY. *Only* CARLOTTA *remains beside* ROBINSON'S *body.*

CLEVELAND (*to* LANE)

Quick, Jemmy, up and over the house-tops!
[*He points to the stairs.*

LANE

Tell 'em to follow me with falcons!
[*He dashes across the room and starts up the steps.*

CLEVELAND

Now, where to stow these two—? (*Turning to* MC-
AULIFFE.) Landlord—?

MCAULIFFE (*in a disgusted tone*)

No, no, no, no! Wait a minute, wait a minute! (*They
all stop their excited movements and stand looking
at* MCAULIFFE *who comes out from behind the bar.*)
There's no use going on this way! (*Calling up the
stairs.*) Come on down again!
[CARLOTTA *rises from her knees.* ROBINSON *and* TOR-
RENCE *rise and brush their clothes.*

LANE (*angrily, as he comes down the steps*)

What's wrong now?

MCAULIFFE

What isn't? It's terrible from start to finish!
[*The others exchange looks of anger and displeasure.*

LANE

I don't see—

MCAULIFFE

You're not expected to—that's my job!

MRS. MONTGOMERY

Really, Mr. McAuliffe—

MCAULIFFE

Now let's all just keep nice and cool. We won't get
anywhere by getting excited. Just pull up a chair
everybody, and make yourselves nice and comfortable.
(*They all form a group in the middle of the stage,
some sitting on stools and chairs, some on tables, and
some standing. Some of the men remove their wigs,*

*and nearly all light cigarettes.* TORRENCE *puts on his glasses.*) Where's the stage-manager? I want him, too!

JESSUP (*jumping up*)

I'll get him! (*He goes to door at Left and calls to someone off-stage.*) Hal!

BRIGGS (*answering from off Left*)

Yes.

JESSUP

You're wanted.

BRIGGS (*still off-stage*)

All right. Right away. (JESSUP *resumes his place, and a moment later* HENRY BRIGGS *enters.*) Anything wrong?

MCAULIFFE (*lighting a cigar*)

Oh no—it's all sweet as May-time. Only—where were those off-stage shots?

BRIGGS

The pistols didn't work.

MCAULIFFE (*his tone caustic throughout*)

So, they didn't work, eh? Six o'clock on the evening of the performance and the pistols don't work—! Did they get damp, and mildew set in?

BRIGGS

My fault, I guess. I forgot to reload them.

MCAULIFFE

Well, that's a fairly good explanation for 'em not going off. It's one of the best I ever heard! What do you suppose a show has a stage-manager for? Just to give the printers something to put on the program? Isn't the list of patronesses long enough?

BRIGGS

I thought it being only a rehearsal—

MCAULIFFE

Yeah—an' tonight'll be only the performance! So for the sake of sweet charity, and the Cope Valley Hospital sinking fund, or whatever it is—

MRS. MONTGOMERY

Mr. McAuliffe, are we to understand that you are not in sympathy with the purpose of this production?

MCAULIFFE

Oh no, Mrs. Montgomery—no indeed. I like hospitals —I was born in one.

[MRS. MONTGOMERY *turns angrily away.*

CARLOTTA (*exclaims in contempt*)

Heavens, what a man!

BRIGGS

The pistols will be all right tonight.

MCAULIFFE

I'd hate to make book on it.

LANE (*sharply*)

You're not obliged to, are you?

ROBINSON

Just a minute! I think all our nerves are a bit frayed by the intensive work we've been doing. So let's stick to business and leave personalities out of it.

MCAULIFFE (*with heavy sarcasm*)

Oh, pardon me, I thought *I* was the director of this show!

ROBINSON

You are, Mr. McAuliffe—and *just* that.

MCAULIFFE

Then maybe I'm not allowed to ask you what happened to *your* gun? And what the idea is, of turning around and throwing up your arm when you're supposed to be fighting a duel?

MRS. MONTGOMERY

I noticed that myself, Hancock.
[*Several of the others murmur assent.*

ROBINSON

It was purely involuntary. The fact is, I didn't like the way that damned gun was pointing at me.

LANE

Where do you expect me to point it? At the ceiling? I'm supposed to send a ball into your chest.

ROBINSON

Don't get excited, old boy. All I said was that I don't like that damned gun pointing at my heart. We all have our little peculiarities. That's mine.

MCAULIFFE

We're giving a performance at eight-thirty tonight —maybe.

ROBINSON

We'll give a performance!

MCAULIFFE

I hope so!

MRS. MONTGOMERY

Is there anything else, Mr. McAuliffe? I have people for tea.

MCAULIFFE

Oh my God.

MRS. MONTGOMERY

I beg your pardon?

MCAULIFFE

Mrs. Montgomery, if you don't want 'em to laugh out loud tonight, you'd better let me get this gun business straight.

MRS. MONTGOMERY

By all means, let's do whatever is necessary. However, we *should* like to finish as quickly as possible.

DR. GRACE

Yes, rather.
*[Murmurs of assent from the others.*

MCAULIFFE

All I'm trying to do is put on your show for you. (*Turning and facing out towards the auditorium*) Where's Maria?

MARIA (*speaking from the rear of the auditorium*)

Yes sir, coming.
*[*MARIA SCOTT *enters, hurrying down the aisle from the rear of the auditorium. She wears nose glasses, has a pencil stuck in her hair, and carries a large*

*black leather-covered loose-leaf notebook.* MCAULIFFE
*and* BRIGGS *help her to climb upon the stage.*

MCAULIFFE

Maria, I want you to see to it personally before we
ring up tonight, that all these guns are loaded.

MARIA

Yes, sir.

BRIGGS

I assure you—

MCAULIFFE (*ignoring him*)

How many guns have we got?

MARIA

Four, besides the four that you bring on with you.

MCAULIFFE

All right. You examine all the guns, and give the four
extra ones to the stage-manager yourself. Got it?

MARIA

Yes sir. And—

MCAULIFFE (*cutting her off*)

One thing at a time. (*To* BRIGGS.) Now about those
shots—they'll have to come earlier.

BRIGGS

Earlier?

MCAULIFFE

Yes. I want the volley from the Guards off-stage at
the same time as the shots in the duel. We've got to
have that duel absolutely covered, in case one of the

guns hangs fire—or somebody gets an attack of temperament. As long as we have plenty of shots we'll be all right. The audience'll be too excited to know where the shots come from.

MRS. MONTGOMERY

Our audience is rather more intelligent than the common run, I think.

MCAULIFFE

Bunk, Mrs. Montgomery.

MRS. MONTGOMERY

I beg your pardon?

MCAULIFFE

I said "bunk"! Audiences are all alike—they never know or care how a thing happens, so long as it happens. But if you have two guys fighting a duel, and the guns don't make some *little* pop, even an audience is liable to think it's phoney—especially when one of the said guys falls down wounded.

BRIGGS (*anxiously*)

But, how will I know—

MCAULIFFE

Easy enough, if you pay attention to what I tell you. All you have to do is count three after Black Tom, there (*pointing to* CLEVELAND) finishes counting the paces. One, two, three, fire! Like that, see?

BRIGGS

I see.

MCAULIFFE

Congratulations. (*Turning to Lane and Robinson.*)
The same thing goes for Jemmy and the Earl—after
six you count three before you fire. Look—(*Taking one of the guns he takes the position of Lane and
begins to count and pace.*) One, two, three, four, five,
six. Seven, turn. Eight, aim. Nine, trigger. Bang!
Do you get it?

LANE and ROBINSON (*together*)

Yes.

MCAULIFFE (*to* BRIGGS)

And after three, *you* fire. Two shots, and then two
more. Get it?

BRIGGS

I've got it.

MCAULIFFE

Splendid. We'll walk through it now. Never mind
loading the guns. I just want to get the timing right.
(LANE *and* ROBINSON *take their former positions in
the middle of the stage, back to back, pistols in hand.*)
MCAULIFFE *continues to* BRIGGS *who has started to
go off-stage.*) No, you stay here and watch their
positions and give me hand-claps for the guns. Now
then—One, two, three, four, five, six. Turn! Aim!
Trigger!

[*As he counts* LANE *and* ROBINSON *go through the
business he has indicated.*

LANE and ROBINSON (*together*)

Bang!

[*At the same instant* BRIGGS *sharply claps his hands twice, then twice again.*

MCAULIFFE

Good! That's the way we'll do it!

MRS. MAXWELL (*impatiently*)

May we go now?

MCAULIFFE

Just a minute, please. (*To* MARIA) What notes have you got there, Maria? (ROBINSON *and* LANE *resume their places and the* OTHERS *shift about impatiently as* MARIA *opens her black notebook*) Just hit the high spots.

MARIA

Well, in the first place, Mr. Torrence was late on his entrance again.

TORRENCE

I know. I'm sorry—it's on account of being so darn near-sighted—I always pull up before I run down the steps. I don't suppose I could wear my glasses, could I?

MCAULIFFE

Eighteenth Century Harold Lloyd? You'll be all right. Anticipate your cue a little and come in as fast as you can.

TORRENCE

I'll do my best.

MCAULIFFE

Angels can do no more! What next?

MARIA

When Mr. Robinson took his gloves off, he threw them on the floor instead of putting them on the bar.

MCAULIFFE

I meant to speak of that.

ROBINSON

What difference does it make where I put my gloves?

MCAULIFFE

It makes a lot of difference. A gentleman doesn't throw his gloves on the floor.

ROBINSON

Who told you that, Mr. McAuliffe?

MCAULIFFE (*furiously*)

Say, listen—(*He stops and composes himself.*) I'm sorry, Mr. Robinson, Esquire, but we want to play this the way it's written. The business calls for him to put his gloves on the bar.

ROBINSON

He's about to fight a duel with a desperado, in which it's more than likely he'll be killed. He's hardly thinking about his gloves at that moment.

MCAULIFFE

That's just what he would be thinking of. He doesn't want to let on that he's afraid. He's putting up a bluff.

MRS. MONTGOMERY

Aren't we wasting time over a very unimportant detail?

MCAULIFFE

It's details that make a performance.

CLEVELAND

Robin, what's the difference *where* you put your gloves?

ROBINSON

None at all. Only—

CLEVELAND

Well then, put them on the bar, and let's get on.

ROBINSON

Certainly. (*To* MCAULIFFE.) Is there any one spot on the bar that seems to you to be more psychologically correct than another?

MCAULIFFE

My good fellow, *I* didn't write this play!

ROBINSON

May I ask you to refrain from calling me your "good fellow"?

MCAULIFFE

"My bad actor," then. Is that all right?

ROBINSON

Are you going to rehearse this play, or are you not?

CLEVELAND

Take it easy, Robin.

MCAULIFFE

That's what I'm here for. And so long as I'm doing

it, you're going to play the part the way I tell you. Can you digest that?

ROBINSON

Look here, McAuliffe, you'll either drop that tone instantly, or——

MCAULIFFE

Or, what——?

MRS. MONTGOMERY

Please! Please!

CLEVELAND

Stop it, Robin.

DR. GRACE

Are we going to be kept here indefinitely?

MRS. MAXWELL

I was about to ask that myself.

ROBINSON

Very well. (*Turning suddenly to Mrs. Montgomery.*) But I want it distinctly understood, Alice, that if I am to continue my connection with the Cope Valley Players, it's this man's last year as director. I've tolerated his bad manners five years too long as it is.

MCAULIFFE

It suits me all right. I've had all I want of amateurs for awhile. I'd rather train seals. When you tell seals something they understand you.

DR. GRACE (*laughs*)

Oh come on—we're acting like a lot of children. Before we know it we'll be calling the whole thing off.

ROBINSON

I'd be just as well pleased if we did. It's not precisely
my idea of a good time to jump from the stage into
my clothes, and go tearing down to New York just
in time to make a dash for the gang-plank of the
*Berengaria*.

MRS. MONTGOMERY

That's nonsense, Hancock. You know you'll have time
to spare.

MCAULIFFE

Nobody ever knew me to walk out on a show. I've
been in this game thirty years, and never had a real
run-in with anyone yet. Shall we go?

DR. GRACE

Let's—by all means.

MCAULIFFE

Places!
[*They all move to take their places.*

MARIA

I beg pardon, Mr. McAuliffe—there's another thing.
[*There are groans of impatience and disgust.*

MCAULIFFE

Well, what is it? Quick! Let's have it!

MARIA

It's just after Mr. Torrence's entrance. Mr. Torrence has fallen and the others have all crossed to
where he lies, leaving Miss Maxwell kneeling beside

Mr. Robinson, who has presumably been rendered unconscious by a bullet-wound—

MCAULIFFE

Yes, yes! What about it?

MARIA

At that point, Mr. Robinson quite visibly caressed Miss Maxwell, which I think rather destroys the illusion.
[*There is an outburst of shocked indignation.*

MRS. MAXWELL (*involuntarily*)

Carlotta!

CARLOTTA

Why, this is the most absurd—
[*The* OTHERS *are obviously embarrassed.*

CLEVELAND

I'm afraid Miss Scott has a vicarious taste for the romantic.

ROBINSON

Look here, Miss Scott—this is a play to be given by ladies and gentlemen, before an audience of ladies and gentlemen, for a deserving charity. Ever since we began rehearsals, it seems to me that you two— (*Including* MCAULIFFE.) have busied yourselves chiefly in stirring up bad feeling among the members of the cast—chiefly between the members of the cast, and *me*.

MARIA

Why, Mr. Robinson!

ROBINSON

What's your game, McAuliffe? Are you doing a little detective work as a side line?

MCAULIFFE

Don't make me laugh!

MARIA

The very idea! I simply take notes on what I see.

MRS. MONTGOMERY (*attempting to dismiss the incident*)

Miss Scott merely made an error in observation. I'm certain that she will——

MARIA

I assure you, I saw it.

MCAULIFFE

Maria never makes mistakes in observation.

LANE (*suddenly bursting out*)

She didn't that time, at any rate!

CARLOTTA (*turning on him angrily*)

What do you mean by such a thing?

MRS. MAXWELL

Carlotta—please—

CARLOTTA (*to* LANE)

Who gave you the right to comment on *my* actions?

LANE

I—
[*He turns away wretchedly.*

ROBINSON

Carlotta—(*She turns to him.*) Let's let it go.

CARLOTTA

All right, just as you say, Robin.

LANE (*wheeling about furiously*)

Why do you call him "Robin"? Why do you? Do you think you're the sparrow that's made a killing? (*He turns to* ROBINSON.) Target practice, is it? If so, I'd like my innings! I'll—

MRS. MAXWELL

Dickie!

LANE

—I'm sorry. I guess I just lost my head.
[*He turns suddenly and goes out. There is an embarrassed silence.*

JESSUP

I'm afraid Dickie's had about two drinks too many. I'll go look after him.
[*He goes out after Lane. There is another embarrassed silence.*

ROBINSON (*finally breaking the silence*)

Well, this settles it.

MCAULIFFE (*quickly*)

Places!

ROBINSON

Just a moment, please! (ALL *turn and look at him. He continues with affected nonchalance.*) I'm sorry good people, to throw another wrench into the machinery, but if I'm going to perform in this play tonight someone other than Dickie Lane will have to stand opposite me in the duel scene.

MCAULIFFE

What's that?

ROBINSON

*That's* that.

MRS. MONTGOMERY

Now Hancock—really—

ROBINSON

I can't help it, Alice. There's a look in that boy's eyes I don't like. He's been drinking, and he's taken it into his head that he has a grievance against me, and—the plain fact is that I don't relish the idea of standing up and being shot at by Dickie Lane.
[*Murmurs of astonishment and incredulity.*

CARLOTTA

Robin!

BRIGGS

We only put blanks in the guns.

ROBINSON

I understand all that, but accidents sometimes happen, you know. A ball might find its way into that gun—and subsequently into my chest. And admitting that good Americans when they die go to Paris, I'd prefer to get there by the more conventional *Berengaria.*

DR. GRACE

Surely you don't think seriously that Dickie—

ROBINSON

Oh no—I'm only expounding my peculiar ideas about guns and accidents.

MRS. MONTGOMERY

You've accused Dickie Lane of harboring murderous thoughts, and I don't think it's very nice of you, I really don't.

ROBINSON

My dear girl, I've accused Dickie Lane of nothing— except drinking and holding a fancied grievance against me. In the circumstances, I prefer not to stand opposite him when he's pointing a gun at me. I'm sorry to be arbitrary about it, but if you're counting on me to perform tonight, somebody else will have to play the part of the amiable bandit chieftain. That's final, I'm afraid. And now if you'll excuse me, I'll go and get a drink myself.
[*He starts to move Right.*

MRS. MONTGOMERY

You might have told us sooner.

ROBINSON

I'm sorry, but I didn't have that feeling about it until just now. There's still time to get somebody else up in the part. I'll be in my dressing-room if you want me.
[*He goes out.*

MRS. MONTGOMERY (*angrily*)

I've never in my life heard anything so ridiculous!

CLEVELAND

I think Robin's perfectly right.

MRS. MAXWELL

You don't, Julian!

CLEVELAND

It happens I do!

MCAULIFFE

Well, folks, once upon a time there was a play in rehearsal—

DR. GRACE

Has anyone any suggestions?

MCAULIFFE

The Ringling Brothers' winter home is in Bridgeport —we might get a couple of elephants over—

MRS. MONTGOMERY

Seriously please, Mr. McAuliffe! Would it be possible to substitute somebody now?

CARLOTTA

It's not a very big part.

MCAULIFFE

How about you, Mr. Briggs? Do you think you could do it?

BRIGGS

I'd rather not, Mr. McAuliffe. I've never acted in my life. I'm afraid I'd make an awful mess of it.

MCAULIFFE

Once you lose 'em, it's awful hard to get 'em back. How about you, Mr. Torrence?

TORRENCE (*with an embarrassed laugh*)

Well, I don't mind trying it. Only—
[*He stops.*

MCAULIFFE

Only what?

TORRENCE (*rather embarrassed*)

Well—I daresay you've all noticed it, so there's no reason for my not mentioning it. (*Almost whispering the rest of the speech.*) My own relations with Mr. Robinson are none too friendly. He may have the same objection to me.

CARLOTTA

Don't be a fool, Clarke!

CLEVELAND

That's absurd, Torrence!

TORRENCE

Well, just as you say. But of course I'm not a crack shot like Dickie Lane. *I* haven't a medal to my name.
[*He laughs.*

MRS. MONTGOMERY

What is the matter with all you people this afternoon? I've never heard such nonsensical talk.

TORRENCE

Mr. Robinson says it's Miss Scott that's to blame. How about that, Miss Scott?

MARIA

I don't know what he could have meant.

TORRENCE

All right, but wait a minute—what about *my* part?

MCAULIFFE

We'll let Lane play it. It's only one side. He can get up in it in ten minutes.

BRIGGS

Dickie may not like giving up his part.

MRS. MAXWELL

Oh, he won't mind. (*Suddenly*) Unless—(*She stops short, the others look at her. She exclaims:* Nothing!

TORRENCE

I think I know most of his lines, but I'd like to look them over.

MCAULIFFE

Yes, sure. (*To* MARIA.) Tell the others to come on stage, and bring Mr. Lane's part.

MARIA

Yes sir.
[*She goes out.*

MRS. MAXWELL

Are we going to rehearse any more?

MCAULIFFE

Just the duel scene, now. I want to get that set.

BRIGGS

Do you want the effects?

MCAULIFFE

Yes. Load the guns, and let Maria inspect them.

BRIGGS

All right.
[*He picks up the guns, and bustling off, exits with them.*

MRS. MONTGOMERY

Mr. McAuliffe, if you don't mind my saying so, that Miss Scott of yours is a very fussy, meddlesome person.

MCAULIFFE

She's trained to be. She's got the all-seeing eye, that girl.

MRS. MONTGOMERY

She seems to cherish a hearty dislike for all of us— do you suppose she could be a Red?

MCAULIFFE

I don't know anything about her politics. I do know she's the best assistant I ever had. Nothing gets away from her.

MRS. MONTGOMERY

*I* liked that little Miss Clinton you had two or three years ago. What became of her?

DR. GRACE

Yes, so did I. What happened to Miss Clinton?

MCAULIFFE (*as* ROBINSON *enters*)

She went away somewhere. I haven't got time to keep track of girls after I'm through with them.

ROBINSON

Well, what have you decided?

CLEVELAND

Torrence is going to play Lane's part.

TORRENCE (*half satirically*)

If that's agreeable to you?

ROBINSON (*lightly*)

Yes, quite.

LANE (*enters in his street clothes, carrying a type-written part in his hand*)

What's this about changing parts?

TORRENCE

You and I are going to shift, Dickie.

LANE

What's the point?

MCAULIFFE (*maliciously*)

The gun-point. Mr. Robinson got the idea you might bump him off in the duel scene.

ROBINSON

Shut up, you fool!
[*Exclamations of indignation from the* OTHERS.

LANE (*to* ROBINSON)

Oh? What gave you that idea?

ROBINSON

Don't be an idiot, Lane. Can't you recognize the man's crude attempt at humor?

TORRENCE (*quickly*)

I asked for the shift, Dickie. I can't make that entrance down the stairs properly on account of my eyes. So I thought you wouldn't mind changing with me——

LANE

Oh sure, that's all right. It's all one to me.
[*He hands the part to* TORRENCE *who begins studying it.* MARIA *enters with the pistols which are used in the duel scene.*

MCAULIFFE

Are they loaded?

MARIA

Yes, sir—and I've inspected them all.
[JESSUP *enters.*

MCAULIFFE

Has Briggs got the others?

MARIA

Yes.

MCAULIFFE

Good! (*To* LANE.) Do you know your business now?

LANE

Yes, I guess so.

MCAULIFFE

On Black Tom's line, "Clear through, east to west. He breathes, though." you open the door, run down the steps, read your line, "The Guard! The Guard!"—whatever it is——

TORRENCE (*looking up from his part*)

"The Guard! The Guard! Did you hear that volley?
Jemmy! For thy life!"

MCAULIFFE

That's it. You say that as you come down the steps,
and then you do your fall about here. Get it?

LANE

Yes, I understand.

MCAULIFFE

Give me that piece of chalk, Maria. (*She hands him
a piece of chalk from her pocket, and he marks the
position on the stage.*) Fall right here—all right.
Then there's just the short scene with the girl in the
third act. We'll run over that a couple of times before the performance tonight.

LANE

Very well.

MCAULIFFE

Now—to run through this duel scene. In your places,
everybody. (*Calling.*) Are you ready with the guns,
stage-manager?

BRIGGS (*off-stage*)

Yes, all ready.

MCAULIFFE (*to* LANE, *as the latter goes up the steps
at Left*)

You be right outside the door there, and open it on
"East to west." Don't wait.

LANE

All right.

[*He goes out through the door at the head of steps.*
[MCAULIFFE *starts to move in the direction of the bar.*

MARIA

I have one more suggestion, Mr. McAuliffe.

MRS. MONTGOMERY

Oh, dear—

MCAULIFFE (*impatiently*)

Well, what is it?

TORRENCE (*grinning*)

Let's all cut each other's throats!

MARIA

I think it would be a good idea for Mr. Robinson to have a sponge full of red ink inside his coat, so that when Mr. Cleveland examines the wound and says, "Clean through, east to west," he holds up his hand and it's all red. When Mansfield—

MCAULIFFE (*impatiently*)

Mansfield, my eye! No phony effects like that! Just get out of the way somewhere, now, and let us play this scene.

[MARIA *gets to an out of the way corner.*

MRS. MONTGOMERY

Oh, for Miss Clinton again.

ROBINSON

Where do we begin?

MCAULIFFE

Take it from where you choose the guns. Here you are—you and Jemmy are in front of the bar. (*To Torrence.*) You'll have to take off that coat. (TORRENCE *removes his coat, showing bare arms.*) Guns! You're upstage, Miss Maxwell—the rest of you take your positions. (*As they comply.*) That's it. Now, about the gloves, Mr. Robinson—let's nail that this time.

ROBINSON

Righto!

[*He picks up the gloves from the floor and puts them on.*

MCAULIFFE

You've picked your gun. "This will do me." Go on from there—

ROBINSON (*turning away, gun in hand*)

"This will do me."

TORRENCE

That's me, isn't it? (*He glances occasionally at the part in his hand.*) Pick up gun. (*He picks up one of the guns.*) "So will this." (*Laughter and murmurs,* TORRENCE *swings around.*) "Spread out, you! Give us a little elbow-room." Is that right?

MCAULIFFE

Good! Yes. Only let it take you over about two feet more. Here—(*He marks the position upon the stage with chalk.* DR. GRACE, MRS. MONTGOMERY, *and* JESSUP *join* CARLOTTA *at Back as before,* CLEVELAND *and* MRS. MAXWELL *down-stage*) There, that's it!

CLEVELAND

"It is agreed between you—six paces, turn and fire?"

TORRENCE

"Agreed!"

[*He strides to the middle of the stage.* ROBINSON *nods.*

ROBINSON

Gloves off—on bar.

MCAULIFFE

That's it.

ROBINSON (*flinging coin on the bar*)

"To pay for your broken crockery, landlord."

JESSUP

"There'll be naught broke, save your wishbone, maybe!" (*Laughter,* MCAULIFFE *pockets the coin.* ROBINSON *to Center,* JESSUP *continues to* CARLOTTA.) "Don't 'e want to see him let the air into thy sweetheart?"

MRS. MONTGOMERY (*slapping* JESSUP *across the mouth*)

"Leave the girl be!"

[JESSUP *goes to Left.* ROBINSON *and* TORRENCE *stand back to back.*

CLEVELAND

"Are you ready?"

TORRENCE

"Ready as rain."

ROBINSON

"I am ready."

CARLOTTA (*rushing to* TORRENCE)

"Oh, I beg thee—beg thee!"

TORRENCE (*pushing her aside*)

"Get off, thou slut! Thou bag of—who'll pluck this leech—(*Referring to his part and turning a page*) —off me?" Sorry, Carlotta.

CARLOTTA (*as* DR. GRACE *and* MRS. MONTGOMERY *pick her up*)

It's all right—I'm used to it by now.

ROBINSON

"Have no fears for me, pretty chick."

CLEVELAND

"Are you ready?"

TORRENCE (*after a moment's pause*)

Oh, I beg your pardon. That's me, isn't it? Just give me that again, will you please?

CLEVELAND

"Are you ready?"

TORRENCE

"Since yesterday, thick-skull!"

ROBINSON

"Give us the count."

CLEVELAND

"One—Two—Three—Four—Five—Six!
[TORRENCE *and* ROBINSON *advance, turn, aim and fire as before. At the same instant five or six shots are heard in rapid succession off-stage Left.*

ROBINSON (*dropping his pistol and staggering forward*)

"God! It caught me! I'm—I'm—"

CARLOTTA

"Harry! Harr-y!"
[*She rushes forward.* DR. GRACE, MRS. MONTGOMERY, CLEVELAND, *and* MRS. MAXWELL *surround* ROBINSON *as before and lower him to stage.*

CLEVELAND (*after examining the body*)

"Clean through, east to west. He breathes, though!"

LANE (*opening entrance door and rushing in and down stairs*)

"The Guard! The Guard! Didst hear that volley? Jemmy—! For thy life!"
[*He falls.* JESSUP, TORRENCE, CLEVELAND, DR. GRACE, MRS. MAXWELL, *and* MRS. MONTGOMERY *surround him, leaving* CARLOTTA *beside* ROBINSON.

CLEVELAND (*to* TORRENCE)

"Quick, Jemmy, up and over the house-tops!"

TORRENCE

"Tell 'em to follow me with falcons!"
[*He rushes across the room in the direction of the steps.*

MCAULIFFE

All right. All right. You're up the steps and off. That's all, that was very good, that time.

MRS. MAXWELL

Well, thank goodness.
[ROBINSON *and* LANE *rise and brush their clothes.*

MCAULIFFE

If we do it that way tonight, they may stay through the second act.

TORRENCE

I'm afraid that—

MCAULIFFE (*holding up his hand*)

Wait a minute, don't start anything.

BRIGGS (*entering, anxiously*)

How were the guns that time? All right?

MCAULIFFE

Yes, very good. Mind you do it the same way tonight.

CARLOTTA

Can we go now?

MCAULIFFE

In just a minute. Did any of you notice anything wrong, that time?

MARIA (*bustling forward*)

Yes, Mr.—

MCAULIFFE (*irritably*)

I'm not asking you, Eagle-eye. Did any of the rest of you see anything wrong?

SEVERAL OF THE OTHERS

Why, no, I didn't notice—
I can't say that I—
It looked all right to me.

MCAULIFFE (*triumphantly*)

Well, that shows you. Here you are, all of you, know

this play from top to bottom. And not one of you
noticed that Jemmy's gun didn't go off.
[*Murmurs of surprise.*

TORRENCE

I'm awfully sorry. I pulled the darned thing as hard
as I could.

MCAULIFFE

It's all right. It's all right. Not your fault. When
you've got trick props to work with, something's
bound to go wrong about one time out of three.
That's why I want those off-stage guns to be right.
Give 'em two shots, and they won't know or care
where they came from, especially the women. Tell
'em there's going to be some shooting, and nine out
of ten of 'em will close their eyes. And the men are
almost as bad.

TORRENCE (*laughs, looks at* MRS. MONTGOMERY *and
says*)

Their eyes'll be closed in sleep by then.

MCAULIFFE

Yeah? Maybe that's true, too—but don't let this
scene buffalo you. I don't want you self-conscious
over it. You play a scene like this with ten characters
in it and a lot of shooting and action, before an
audience of six hundred people and ask everybody
to write down what he saw—and what do you think
you'll get? Six hundred different stories, that's what!
So if afterwards any of you wants to kill the author
of this piece, or the guy who directed it, take my
tip an' don't do it in a dark alley or in the middle of

a desert, because they'll be sure to get you if you do.
Just bump us off in a crowd, in full daylight with
five hundred witnesses—the chances are you'll get
away with it! Now are we all friends again?

ALL TOGETHER

Of course.
Certainly.
I'm sure we're very grateful.

TORRENCE (*fingering his gun amusedly*)

That's a very useful piece of advice. How about it,
Mr. Robinson?

ROBINSON (*laughing*)

Oh, *you* don't worry me, Torrence.

MCAULIFFE

That's all now. Get into your clothes, and we'll meet
here for just a minute before you go.

CARLOTTA

Not more rehearsals!

MCAULIFFE

No, not this afternoon.

MRS. MONTGOMERY (*to* ROBINSON)

Is your car here, Hancock?

ROBINSON

No. Awfully sorry, I was counting on you.

MRS. MONTGOMERY

It's quite all right—

BRIGGS (*to the* OTHERS)

I can take the rest of you.

MRS. MONTGOMERY (*continuing*)

—I just wanted to know. Do you mind telephoning up to Thompson to bring it down?

ROBINSON

Certainly.
[*He goes out at Right.*

JESSUP (*pushing* TORRENCE *from behind*)

"Jemmy! For thy life, boy!"

TORRENCE

"Aye, aye, thick-skull!"—Judas, what a play!
[*They go out at Right.*

CLEVELAND (*answering* BRIGGS)

Thanks. That's fine.
[*He goes out at Right followed by* MRS. MONTGOMERY.

BRIGGS

Anything else for me, Mr. McAuliffe?

MCAULIFFE

Nope! I think we're all set now.

BRIGGS

Righto.
[*He goes out at Left.*

MCAULIFFE (*to* MARIA)

Don't let that electrician get away. I want to go over the light plot with him. I want all the light we can get on that duel, and not so much in the corners.

MRS. MAXWELL (*to* LANE)

You know how I feel, Dickie.

LANE

Thanks.

MCAULIFFE (*continuing to* MARIA)

I want him to dim the borders, and use all the baby-spots.

MARIA

Shall I tell him?

MCAULIFFE

No, you just hold him. I'll be right there myself.

MARIA

Yes sir.

[*She goes out at Left.* CARLOTTA *goes out at Right.*

MCAULIFFE (*going over to* LANE *and taking him by the arm*)

Well, old boy, are you going to feel easy in the new part?

LANE (*impatiently*)

Oh yes, I'll be all right.

MCAULIFFE

I don't blame you, kid. If it was my girl, I'd feel the same way.

LANE

What the hell business is it of yours?

MCAULIFFE

Well, take a tip from an old-timer, and save your hootch until after the show.

LANE

When I want your advice, McAuliffe, I'll ask for it.

MCAULIFFE

Keep your shirt on! Personally, I don't care if you take shoe-polish in your tea.

[*He goes out at Left.* CARLOTTA *enters as* MCAULIFFE *goes.*

LANE (*intercepting* CARLOTTA)

Carlotta!

CARLOTTA (*forced to stop. Impatiently*)

Well, what is it?

LANE

I want to talk to you.

CARLOTTA

I'm dead tired, and I want to get out of these clothes.

LANE

I only want to ask you—

CARLOTTA

Not now, I tell you.

LANE

Afterwards, then. After you're dressed.

CARLOTTA

After I'm dressed, I'm going to go home and lie down.

LANE

Let me take you?

CARLOTTA

Thanks, but I'm going in Hal Briggs' car.

LANE

Why can't you go with me just as well?

CARLOTTA

Because I don't want to. (*Bursting out:*) I think you've been behaving about as rottenly as anyone could!

LANE

If I have, you know why.

CARLOTTA

No—and what's more, I don't give a hang.

LANE

You know it's—only since you stopped caring for me.

CARLOTTA

I never did care for you.
[MRS. MAXWELL *enters up Right.*

LANE

You can stand there and say you never cared for me?

CARLOTTA

Well, maybe I did in a way, once.

LANE

Yes, in a way. Enough to want to marry me—until you lost your head over Robinson.—Robinson!
[*He laughs bitterly.*

CARLOTTA

You can leave him out of it. And you may as well

understand right now, that what I do or don't do is
no concern of yours!

LANE

It is some concern of mine, when you mean everything
in the world to me, and I see you throwing yourself
away on a—

CARLOTTA

That's enough, Dick! (*Pause, she goes to the bar.*)
Good-bye—thanks for being so sweet—once.

LANE

Is that your last word on it?

CARLOTTA

Sorry, Dickie—it's just that. (*He stops short then
turns and goes out abruptly at Left.* CARLOTTA
*covers her face for a moment with her hands.*) Oh!

MRS. MAXWELL (*approaching her*)

Carlotta!

CARLOTTA (*turning*)

Please don't begin all over again, Mother.

MRS. MAXWELL

How can you treat Dickie like that?

CARLOTTA

I treated him better than he deserves—a lot better.

MRS. MAXWELL

Until a month ago, you hadn't a thought for anyone
else.

[DR. GRACE *enters up Right, both look up but continue talking.*

CARLOTTA

I think I have a right to change my mind, if I want to.

MRS. MAXWELL

I don't believe you have changed it. It's been changed for you—by a man who is rather expert at such things.

CARLOTTA

Listen, dear—I'm not quite such a fool as you seem to think I am.

MRS. MAXWELL

You're not as wise as you think you are—that's certain.

DR. GRACE

Carlotta, look here a moment, will you?

CARLOTTA

I'm tired of discussing it, Uncle Ned!

DR. GRACE

It was your father's last wish that I should look out for you, as he himself would. I've tried to fulfill that obligation to the best of my ability.

CARLOTTA (*warmly*)

Oh, don't!

DR. GRACE

I want you to try to see the thing from the outside. How do you think it's going to look—a young girl eloping with a married man twice her age?

CARLOTTA (*indignantly*)

Who says it's eloping?

DR. GRACE

What do you call it, then?

CARLOTTA

Two people happen to sail for Europe on the same boat.

MRS. MAXWELL

You know very well it's not as innocent as that.

CARLOTTA

It is, I tell you.

MRS. MAXWELL

Then why did you try to keep it secret?

CARLOTTA

To avoid this sort of thing! I knew the fuss you'd both make.

DR. GRACE

But why should we object, if it's all as casual as you say it is?

CARLOTTA

I never said it was casual. I've told you that Robin and I are in love with each other.

MRS. MAXWELL

So you run off with him!

CARLOTTA

We happen both to be sailing on the *Berengaria*.

MRS. MAXWELL

Carlotta, we are only trying to save you from great, great unhappiness.

CARLOTTA

I'm the best judge of what's happiness for me, Mother. I'll be all right on the boat, you can rest assured. And we'll be married in Paris, as soon as Robin gets his divorce there.

DR. GRACE

What if he doesn't get it?

CARLOTTA

He will!

DR. GRACE

But suppose he doesn't?

CARLOTTA

I imagine I know how to take care of myself in the meantime.

DR. GRACE

It's not the same thing, Carlotta, talking to us about it, and being off somewhere alone with him.

CARLOTTA

Can't you get rid of the idea that I'm a child?

MRS. MAXWELL (*bursting out*)

You *are* a child—an irresponsible child—or you'd see this man for what he is! He's a libertine—of the worst sort! You aren't the first young girl—

CARLOTTA

Mother! (*A pause.*) You'll please be good enough to take that back!

[MRS. MAXWELL *turns away.*

DR. GRACE

There *are* some ugly stories, Carlotta.

CARLOTTA

Yes—when a man's brilliant and successful, there are always people ready to slander him!

MRS. MAXWELL

The stories about him are not slander, Carlotta.

CARLOTTA

He's told me himself all about that Margaret Wallace affair. That was out-and-out blackmail.

MRS. MAXWELL

Were the others?

CARLOTTA

There haven't been any others!

DR. GRACE

Suppose we gave you evidence?

CARLOTTA

I don't believe you have any!

DR. GRACE

Not at this moment, no. But I will have soon—I've been investigating.

CARLOTTA

Spying?

MRS. MAXWELL

Doesn't it mean anything to you that his own law-partner loathes and detests him?

CARLOTTA

That's not true! Robin and Mr. Cleveland are devoted friends. The fact that Mr. Cleveland's sister married Robin—and they weren't happy—*that* doesn't make any difference to *him*—none at all!

DR. GRACE

Watch Cleveland's face sometime when he's looking at him. They had some kind of discussion in Robinson's dressing-room this afternoon. I saw Cleveland coming out. He was white with rage, and shaking all over.

CARLOTTA

More spying!
[DR. GRACE *turns away.*

MRS. MAXWELL

We'll do anything to keep you from ruining your life.

CARLOTTA

I'm not ruining it. I'm making it!

DR. GRACE

Will you listen to one suggestion, Carlotta—one practical suggestion?

CARLOTTA

What is it?

DR. GRACE

Let Robinson go to Paris, as he plans. Let him get his divorce. After he has it, he can come back and marry you—or if you prefer, you can join him there. Isn't that a better idea?

CARLOTTA

No!

DR. GRACE

Why not? If you really love each other, a few months shouldn't make any difference.

CARLOTTA

We're only happy when we're together. Why should we be apart when we don't have to be?

[*A pause, then* DR. GRACE *turns to* MRS. MAXWELL.

DR. GRACE

I'm afraid it's useless, Helen.

CARLOTTA

Yes, my dears, I'm afraid it is. Don't think I'm not grateful for your concern about me—I am. And don't think I don't hate to leave you in this way—I do. I love you both dearly. But this is bigger than me— or you—or anything. (*With a little gesture.*) And I just don't want to talk about it!

[*She goes out Left. There is a brief silence, then* MRS. MAXWELL *turns to* DR. GRACE *in desperation.*

MRS. MAXWELL

What are we going to do, Edgar? (*He gestures help-lessly.*) Can we stand by, and let her throw her life away?

DR. GRACE

How can we stop her? She has her own money now. You can't make a prisoner of a girl of twenty.

MRS. MAXWELL

We must do something! We must!!

DR. GRACE

What?

MRS. MAXWELL

You go to him! You appeal to him!

DR. GRACE

I have.

MRS. MAXWELL

When?

DR. GRACE

Last night.

MRS. MAXWELL

Why didn't you tell me? What did he say?
[*A pause.*

DR. GRACE

He insisted that Carlotta was quite safe with him.
He knows you and I are helpless—he made that quite
clear. Oh, if we only had the *time* to show her the
sort of bounder he is.

MRS. MAXWELL

They're going away together tonight!

DR. GRACE

I'll do anything to prevent it! Anything!

MRS. MAXWELL

I know, Edgar—but what?
[*A pause.*

DR. GRACE

Something to keep him from sailing, tonight—

MRS. MAXWELL

What?

DR. GRACE

An accident—an injury maybe—! Do you remember what they were saying—about how easy it would be, in the confusion of a crowd-scene, in a play?

MRS. MAXWELL

Tonight?

DR. GRACE

Yes, tonight, during the performance. The scene in the first act—you know, the duel—

MRS. MAXWELL (*tensely*)

Yes.

DR. GRACE

Just after the shot, we're all surrounding him—four or five of us—

[*He stops as* CLEVELAND *enters dressed in street clothes.*

CLEVELAND (*genially, as he sees them*)

Hello! You look like a couple of conspirators.

DR. GRACE

I've been going over that long speech of Helen's with her.

MRS. MAXWELL

At last I've got it straight.

CLEVELAND

I wouldn't worry about it. Aren't you going to change your clothes?

[ROBINSON *and* JESSUP *enter.*

MRS. MAXWELL

I thought I'd just put my coat on over this, and change at home. (*Moving to Right.*) I wonder if Alice has any aspirin—my head's splitting.

DR. GRACE

I'll see.

[*He goes out Right.*

CLEVELAND

I'm getting fed up with this acting business.

ROBINSON

I need six wet days on board ship to set *me* up again.

JESSUP

I envy you.

[MCAULIFFE *enters from Left, smoking a cigarette. The others enter from Right in the following order:* MRS. MONTGOMERY, DR. GRACE, TORRENCE, BRIGGS, *and* CARLOTTA.

MCAULIFFE (*looking them over*)

Everybody here? Where's Mr. Lane?

JESSUP

Dickie went home.

MCAULIFFE (*Anxiously*)

He's not quitting on us, is he?

JESSUP

Oh no, he'll be all right tonight.

MCAULIFFE

All I want to say, is—

MARIA (*entering*)

Mr. McAuliffe.

MCAULIFFE (*cutting her short*)

All I want to say is, folks—once more, don't worry about tonight. Everything's going to be all right. You're going to give a great performance, and don't mind anything I said to you. If I razzed you, it's only because I know that that's the way to handle a troupe on the last day. I'm an old-timer at this game, you know. I've been in show-business thirty years—started with a circus when I was a kid. I've worked in tent shows, and medicine shows, been a vaudeville headliner, and had my own stock company. And I know that the one thing you got to do with an actor is to keep him on his toes until the last minute. All right. Now go on home and eat a good dinner, and get some sleep if you can. And everybody on stage here at seven-thirty, with costumes and make-up.

CARLOTTA

Seven-thirty!

MCAULIFFE

Well, say seven-forty-five. That's all. You do what I tell you, and we'll score a knock-out.

[*The group breaks up, moving to down Left to go out.*

MRS. MONTGOMERY (*moving towards the doorway*)

Who's coming with me? Hancock?

ROBINSON

Yes, if I may.

MRS. MONTGOMERY

Edgar, and Clarke—anybody else?

BRIGGS

I can take the rest—they all go my way.

MRS. MONTGOMERY (*at the door*)

How about you, Mr. McAuliffe? And Miss Scott? Can't I drop you somewhere?

MCAULIFFE

No thanks, Maria and I have got a little work to do yet. (*All except* MCAULIFFE *and* MARIA *go out Left, laughing and chattering.*) MCAULIFFE *sighs wearily.*) Well, let's have the curtain down. I wonder if Jerry's still there? (*He calls.*) Jerry!

A VOICE (*answering from off-stage*)

Yes, sir?

MCAULIFFE (*calling*)

Ring down, will you?

VOICE (*off-stage*)

Yes, sir!

[*There is a final peal of laughter from* MRS. MONT-GOMERY *off Left.* MCAULIFFE *looks disgustedly after the crowd, speaking as the Curtain begins to descend:*

MCAULIFFE

God, what a bunch! I'm glad I don't have to sit out

there and watch 'em tonight. *Some* show, it'll be. Some show!

[*The red draped Curtain of the supposed amateur theatre starts to descend first, and is followed by the regular theatre Curtain.*

CURTAIN

# ACT TWO

# ACT TWO

*Scene: The same stage-setting as Act 1, but now reversed, as if viewed from the back of the stage, showing the back of the red draped curtain, and when it is raised, the blackness of the darkened auditorium beyond.*

*As the setting is now reversed, the sideboard and table used as bar are now at Left, with the door downstage below them. The stairs are now at Right, with the long table beneath. And instead of seeing the back wall of the room we now see the back of the red draped curtain, and at each side the rear of the return wings. At either side on the returns are the upright side-strips of the proscenium arch, shining toward the front. Across the top is seen a pipe with a number of spotlights also shining toward the front. As the red draped curtain is raised there are seen the three long footlight strips, also shining toward front, and the sides of the proscenium arch can be seen. A black drop behind all gives the effect of the darkened auditorium. The footlights, baby-spots, and side-strips are all lighted, as are the two hanging lanterns on the scene. The small tables are now down-stage and the chairs and stools about them are now facing back-stage toward the supposed auditorium.*

*Time: The time is about half past eight the same evening, just before the performance of the play.*

*At Rise: The scene is lighted by the hanging lanterns,*

*and by the rear baby-spots, side-strips, and footlights.*
*Before the Act actually begins, the theatre curtain*
*ascends, disclosing the red draped curtain of the ama-*
*teur stage.* MRS. MONTGOMERY *enters through the center*
*of the curtain to address the audience. She wears an*
*evening wrap over her costume, holding it tightly closed*
*over her bosom. In one hand she holds a program, and*
*a sheet of paper with a typewritten account of ex-*
*penses and proceeds. Her make-up is rather badly done,*
*particularly about the eyes.*

MRS. MONTGOMERY (*addressing the audience*)

Ladies and Gentlemen—Friends—for that is what
you have once more proved yourselves to be—dear
friends of us, the Cope Valley Community Players—
generous friends indeed of the Cope Valley General
Hospital—with your permission I wish to make a
brief announcement, before the performance begins.
First of all, there is a slight mistake in the program.
The part of "Jemmy" will be played by Mr. Clarke
Torrence, and the part of "Dick Tuttle, His Friend"
by Mr. Richard Lane, instead of—er—instead of
vice-versa. Is that clear now? If you will look at your
programs, you will see "Jemmy—Mr. Richard Lane,
Dick Tuttle, His Friend—Mr. Clarke Torrence."
That is a mistake, it should be just the other way
around. Mr. Tuttle—Mr. *Torrence*, that is, takes
the part of "Jemmy", and Mr. Lane, that of "Dick
Tor"—"Dick *Tuttle*," I should say. Also, that the
ginger-ale served in the tavern scene was not furnished by the Easy-Plan Piano Company, but by
Jin-jo-Jem Beverages, Incorporated. It is the piano
which the Easy-Plan Piano Company furnished. Now

then, I think we are all straight so far as the program goes. Well, my dear friends, to an assemblage such as this, a history of the Cope Valley Players is quite unnecessary. Our present production, however, merits a word of explanation. We were so successful the year before last with "It Pays to Advertise," and again last year with "A Pair of Sixes," that this year, following a suggestion made by our director, Mr. McAuliffe, we decided to broaden our sphere of endeavor, and attempt a costume-play. All children like to dress up, you know—and I suppose we're all just grown-up children. For five weeks now, we've been just as busy as bees—rehearsing—trying on costumes—all the hundred-and-one little duties that go with the successsful production of a difficult period-play. I think we can justly point with pride to our record of giving our audiences clean plays, and clean plays only. I trust that you will find this evening's choice no exception in that regard. Of course it is practically impossible to find a period-play without some little bit of spice in it—but there is clean spice, and spice that is not-so-clean. In our selection this evening, I am sure you will meet only the clean spice, and as always, you know "Honi soit qui mal y pense." The financial returns bid fair to be most gratifying. Most. Full returns have not yet been made, but it appears at present that we have beaten our own record of last year. There were some people —and I am afraid I ought to scold them—who *would* pay more than the price stamped on the tickets— and there was the usual generous check from Mr. Patterson—and another from Block Brothers, the coal people. Briefly, the receipts to date from the sale of tickets, advertisements in the program, and donations—$2,387.50. Expenses, including rent of theatre, director's fees, author's royalty,—we did everything we could about that, but it was no use,— costumes, printing, and refreshments which will be served in the lounge after the second act,—$2,274.00. —Leaving a net profit on the evening of $113.50 to which I shall add, with your permission $11.50, in memory of my father, Nicholas Cope, making the total an even $125.00. So I think we may all feel certain that the trees in front of the Nurse's Home will at last have the attention from the Davey Tree Specialists which they have so long needed and which we all have so long desired for them. For the Players and for the Hospital, I thank you from my heart, and wish you all the pleasantest evening imaginable. And now, as they say, "On with the play—let joy be unconfined!"

*[She bows, makes a slight gesture of thanks, and goes out, backwards, through the center of the red curtain. There is a moment's pause, and the red curtain rises disclosing the reversed scene as described. There are discovered, MCAULIFFE who is at Back at the rear of the red curtain looking out through the peephole, BRIGGS who is also by the curtain at Back, DR. GRACE and CLEVELAND who are seated at opposite sides of a table Down Center, and MARIA who with powder puff and pencils is giving the finishing touches to MRS. MAXWELL's make-up. MRS. MONTGOMERY's voice is heard out in front of the red curtain finishing her address to the imaginary audience beyond.*

MRS. MONTGOMERY'S VOICE

—From my heart, and wish you all the pleasantest evening imaginable. And now, as they say, "On with the play—let joy be unconfined!"
[*There is applause from the imaginary audience.* BRIGGS *holds the curtain back for her and she enters, backwards.*

CLEVELAND (*applauding noiselessly*)

Bravo, Alice!

DR. GRACE

Splendid!

MRS. MONTGOMERY

They seemed to take it very well.

MCAULIFFE

Yeah, we've got a lucky break. Looks to me like they'll take anything.
[MRS. MONTGOMERY *gives him a severe look.*

MRS. MONTGOMERY

I'm glad that Colonel Wadsworth was able to get here. He's sitting—
[MARIA *unexpectedly jabs her face with the powder-puff.*

MCAULIFFE

All right, Maria, that'll do! We may as well get all the laughs we can.

BRIGGS

All ready?

MCAULIFFE

Yes, let's go! House lights out, and ring up when the singing starts.

BRIGGS

Right!
[*He goes hastily out.*

MCAULIFFE

Places, everybody! (MRS. MAXWELL *seats herself upon* CLEVELAND'S *knee.* MRS. MONTGOMERY *moves to a position behind the bar.* MCAULIFFE *suddenly wheels on her.*) Take off that wrap!

MRS. MONTGOMERY (*nervously, taking off the wrap*)

Oh my goodness, I almost forgot! Wouldn't that have been awful!

MARIA

I'll take it.
[*She takes the wrap and goes out, hastily.*

MCAULIFFE (*taking up a long stemmed pipe and standing behind the table*)

All right, now! One—two—three—
[DR. GRACE *begins bawling out an Eighteenth Century drinking-song.* MCAULIFFE *waves his pipe to the rhythm.* CLEVELAND *beats time with his empty ale-mug.* MRS. MONTGOMERY, *behind the bar begins washing mugs. The rear curtain slowly rises.*
[*Beyond is seen the darkened auditorium, and applause is heard from the off-stage audience. The spot-and footlights go on.* MRS. MONTGOMERY *smiles and bows her acknowledgment. The singing continues. At*

*the end of each verse,* CLEVELAND, MCAULIFFE, *and* MRS. MAXWELL *join vociferously in the chorus.* DR. GRACE *grows hoarser and hoarser.*

MRS. MAXWELL

What ails thee, lad? Thou'rt croaking like a love-lorn frog.

CLEVELAND

He hath need to wet his whistle.

DR. GRACE

Aye, that I have.

CLEVELAND (*thumping on the table with his mug*)

Ale, Ben, ale!

MCAULIFFE (*without stirring*)

Aye, aye. (*Bawling at* MRS. MONTGOMERY.) Dost hear, woman?

MRS. MONTGOMERY

Hear what?

MCAULIFFE

If thine ears were half so long as thy tongue, thou'd have no need to ask. (*He bellows.*) Ale!

MRS. MONTGOMERY

Thou canst fetch it thyself, thy legs being not near so short as thy wit.

[*A roar of laughter from the others at* MCAULIFFE'S *expense.* MRS. MONTGOMERY *looks out and smiles at the off-stage audience.*

MCAULIFFE (*bellowing*)

Bestir thyself, woman!

MRS. MONTGOMERY

I have been told bestir thyself, these twenty years now—yet am I just where I was.
[*Laughter from the rest.*

MCAULIFFE (*grumblingly, picking up the empty mugs*)

A pox on all women, say I! (*He goes to the bar with the mugs and thumps them down upon it.*) Ale, Vinegar-face. Ale, thou— (*The entrance door opens and* JESSUP *enters amid applause from the off-stage audience, which is renewed with each succeeding entrance.* MCAULIFFE *sees him.*) Hi! Look, will you! Bob Steele —and without a wench!

DR. GRACE (*turning and calling*)

Hi, Bob!

JESSUP (*as he comes down the steps*)

Well met, lads, I've news for ye.

CLEVELAND

Thou'st not turned honest, perchance?

JESSUP

Nay, I've no wish to lose thy friendship.
[*He goes to table, claps* DR. GRACE *on the shoulder, and then with mock gallantry kisses* MRS. MAXWELL'S *hand.*

DR. GRACE (*calling*)

Ale for Bob, Ben!

MCAULIFFE

Aye! (*To* MRS. MONTGOMERY.) Ale for Bob!

CLEVELAND

And one for thyself, Ben.

MRS. MONTGOMERY (*as she refills the mugs*)

Use it to drink thyself in thy grave!

MCAULIFFE

Nay, for thou wouldst come and lie beside me, even there.
[*Laughter from the others.*

MRS. MONTGOMERY (*a little embarrassed over this line*)

And as ever, 'twould not disturb thy sleep.
[*There is a roar of laughter from the others.* MC-AULIFFE, *muttering to himself, carries the five filled mugs over to the table.*

CLEVELAND (*to* JESSUP)

Well, what's thy news, Lad?

JESSUP

'Twill make thee open thy ears.

DR. GRACE

Out with it, then!

JESSUP (*as* MCAULIFFE *distributes the mugs*)

There's a price been put on Jemmy's head. (*Ex-clamations of surprise and consternation. They are now all quite sober and attentive.* MRS. MONTGOMERY *comes from behind the bar, and joins the group at the table.*) A hundred sovereigns, dead or alive!

CLEVELAND (*banging his fist*)

Damn their souls!

DR. GRACE

Where is the lad?

JESSUP

He's fled to Westborn Wood. (CARLOTTA *enters, and comes down the stairs at Back. She stops on the landing to listen, as yet unobserved by the others.* JESSUP *continues to* MCAULIFFE.) 'Tis the work of your fine-spoken gentleman!

CLEVELAND (*in astonishment*)

Lord Harry?

JESSUP

Aye, none other. (*Exclamations of surprise and anger. He continues to* MCAULIFFE.) This comes of letting thy daughter consort with gentry.
[*Murmurs of assent from the others.*

MRS. MONTGOMERY

Leave Meg out of it!

CARLOTTA (*defiantly, as she comes down the steps*)

If anyone has aught to say, let him speak!
[*All turn and look hastily at her.*

MRS. MONTGOMERY

Go to thy room!

CARLOTTA

I'll not go to my room. (*To* JESSUP.) Well, say what thou hast to say.

JESSUP

There's a price set on Jemmy's head.

MRS. MAXWELL

And, 'tis the doing of that fine lord, thy lover!

CARLOTTA (*angrily*)

I have no lover, and I know no lord!

DR. GRACE

Hear the girl!

CLEVELAND

Who is he, then—your gentleman-in-waiting?

CARLOTTA

A gentleman. What then? 'Tis no crime to be a gentleman.

DR. GRACE

Why does he come here?

CARLOTTA

'Tis a public-house, is't not? Whoever can pay his reckoning can come or go as please him.

JESSUP (*fingering his dagger significantly*)

He may go out heels first, as a warning to others of his kind.
[*Murmurs of approval.*

CARLOTTA

If any one of you—

MRS. MONTGOMERY

Hold thy tongue, girl!

JESSUP (*to* CARLOTTA, *pushing* MRS. MONTGOMERY *aside*)

Well, what? If anyone of us—?
[*The entrance door opens.*

CLEVELAND (*as he sees the door open, warningly*)

Wait a moment, Bob.
[*They all look towards the entrance door as* ROBIN-
SON *appears at the head of the steps. He hesitates
for a moment as he senses the hostility, then with
affected nonchalance comes down the steps.*

ROBINSON (*to the assembled company as he comes down
the steps*)

Good evening, good folk.
[*There is a silence finally broken by* CARLOTTA.

CARLOTTA

Good evening, sir.

ROBINSON (*seating himself at a table near the door
apart from the others*)

A glass of sherry, my lass.

CARLOTTA

Aye sir, with pleasure sir.
[*She goes to the bar covertly eyeing the group about
the table as she goes.* MRS. MONTGOMERY *hurries after
her and tries in inaudible tones to persuade her to go
upstairs.* CARLOTTA *persistently refuses and freeing
herself goes behind the bar and pours the wine. The
group about the table is engaged in sullen whispering.
As* CARLOTTA *comes from behind the bar* MRS. MONT-
GOMERY *intercepts her again.*

MRS. MONTGOMERY (*trying to take the wine from* CAR-
LOTTA)

I'll serve the gentleman.

CARLOTTA

Don't trouble thyself.

ROBINSON

'Tis your daughter's fair hand that gives your sherry
its rare flavor, landlady.

CLEVELAND (*boldly*)

Everything has its price, m'lord.

CARLOTTA (*angrily*)

That's enough, Black Tom!

ROBINSON

You mistake me, sir. I am no lord—merely a gentleman with a taste for wine.

[*There are growls of incredulity, and jeering.* CAR-
LOTTA *sets the glass down beside* ROBINSON, *and in a
whisper warns him that he is in danger.* ROBINSON
*merely smiles and tries to take her hand in his. She
tries to withdraw her hand, repeating her warning,
but he holds it fast. The others are watching atten-
tively with increasing hostility. Suddenly* MRS. MAX-
WELL, *who has been looking in the direction of the
entrance door, springs to her feet.*

MRS. MAXWELL (*as the door opens and* TORRENCE *enters*)

Jemmy!

[*She points to the door, the others jump to their
feet and stand in amazement looking at* TORRENCE

*who stands at the head of the steps with folded arms,
looking fixedly at* ROBINSON, *who is still holding* CAR-
LOTTA's *hand. She snatches her hand away but stands
close beside* ROBINSON. TORRENCE *comes slowly down
the steps.*

JESSUP (*rushing towards him*)

Jemmy, art mad? What dost thou here?

TORRENCE (*without taking his eyes from* ROBINSON)

I've some private business with yon gentlemen.

JESSUP

'Tis no safe place for thee.

TORRENCE

Dick Tuttle is on the watch. And safety is for old
women. (*As* TORRENCE *approaches,* ROBINSON *slowly
rises and faces him, his hand on his sword hilt. The
others edge in nearer. Standing before* ROBINSON *with
a mocking smile, his arms folded,* TORRENCE *continues.*) Well, my lord, I've come to put a round hundred golden sovereigns within reach of your paw.

ROBINSON

You mistake me, my man. I know not who you are,
nor what you mean.

TORRENCE

Then I'll speak a language that translates itself—
[*He takes* ROBINSON's *glass and dashes the wine into
his face.*

ROBINSON (*raging*)

Thief! Scoundrel! Gallows-bird!
[*He draws his sword, but* JESSUP *seizes his arm, while*

CLEVELAND *and* DR. GRACE, *each with a dagger in his hand, seize him from behind.* TORRENCE *stands opposite him as before, smiling mockingly.*

JESSUP

Shall we finish him, Jemmy?

TORRENCE

Wouldst rob me of the pleasure, Bob?

ROBINSON

I warn you that if any harm befalls me, within the week you'll all swing on a gallows-tree!

TORRENCE (*to* MCAULIFFE)

Pistols, Ben!

MCAULIFFE

Aye, Jemmy, aye.
[*He bustles across stage and goes out Left.*

ROBINSON

Again I tell you—

TORRENCE

Enough! I give you more than you deserve—a chance to save your skin. (*To the* OTHERS.) Turn him loose, lads, and clear the room! (*They release* ROBINSON, *who goes to the bar and stands with one elbow leaning on it.* DR. GRACE, CLEVELAND, JESSUP, MRS. MAXWELL, *and* MRS. MONTGOMERY *begin moving chairs and tables aside.* CARLOTTA *stands to one side, uncertain as to her course.*) What dost think, Black Tom, six paces?

CLEVELAND

It is customary. (*Calling to* ROBINSON.) Dost hear?
Six paces!
[ROBINSON *does not answer.*

CARLOTTA (*approaching* TORRENCE *timidly*)

Jemmy, I beg thee—

TORRENCE

Harlot!
[*He spits upon the floor at her feet, and turns his
back on her. She turns to the rear of the room, sinks
on one of the stools, and flinging her arms across the
table buries her head in them. The grouping is now as
at the opening of the First Act*—ROBINSON *standing
at the bar,* CARLOTTA *seated at the table,* TORRENCE
*standing Center with folded arms,* CLEVELAND, DR.
GRACE, JESSUP, MRS. MAXWELL, *and* MRS. MONTGOM-
ERY *whispering together nearby.* MCAULIFFE *enters
at Left with the pistols.*

MCAULIFFE (*going behind the bar and putting down the
pistols.*)

There, my fighting cocks—I give my guests what
they demand. Pistols be out of season, but here you
have 'em!

CLEVELAND (*pulling* TORRENCE *by the arm*)

Come, Jemmy—praying won't steady thy hand any.

TORRENCE (*wrenching his arm free*)

Praying? Me? *He's* the one needs prayers.
[*He goes to the bar beside* ROBINSON. *All the others
but* CARLOTTA *form a tense group around them.*

ROBINSON (*to* TORRENCE)

Will you choose?

TORRENCE (*with a mocking bow*)

After you, m'lord.

ROBINSON (*angrily*)

I'm a commoner like yourself, do you understand?

TORRENCE

Yes, m'lord—or more so.
[*There is a titter of laughter.* ROBINSON *turns to examining the pistols, and finally decides upon one.*

ROBINSON (*turning away with the pistol*)

This will do me.
[*Without a second's hesitation* TORRENCE *picks up a pistol. There are murmurings and nudgings among the others.*

TORRENCE

So will this.
[*He turns away, but forgets to read his next line. There is a moment's awkward pause, as the others wait for the cue.*

MCAULIFFE (*jumping in, speaking quickly*)

Give the lad a little elbow room.
[*The others respond to the cue,* DR. GRACE, MRS. MONTGOMERY, *and* JESSUP *going up-stage near* CARLOTTA, CLEVELAND *and* MRS. MAXWELL *remaining down-stage at the end of the bar.*

CLEVELAND

It is agreed between you—six paces, turn and fire?

TORRENCE

Agreed!

[ROBINSON *nods.* TORRENCE *strides to the middle of the stage.* ROBINSON *takes off his gloves, throws one on the floor, then remembering that he is to put them on the bar, stoops and picks it up as though it had been an accident and places both gloves on the bar. He then takes a coin from his pocket.*

ROBINSON (*flinging the coin on the bar*)

To pay for your broken crockery, landlord.

JESSUP

There'll be naught broke save your wishbone, maybe. (*Jeering laughter.* MCAULIFFE *pockets the coin.* ROBINSON *goes to Center.* JESSUP *nudges* CARLOTTA.) Don't ye want to see him let the air into thy sweetheart?

MRS. MONTGOMERY (*slapping* JESSUP *across the mouth*)

Leave the girl be!

[JESSUP *goes to Left.* ROBINSON *and* TORRENCE *take up their positions back to back at Center.*

CLEVELAND

Are you ready?

[TORRENCE *forgets his line again, and there is another moment's awkward pause.*

MCAULIFFE (*quickly*)

Be you ready, Jemmy?

TORRENCE (*startled*)

Aye, aye!

CARLOTTA (*suddenly rushing up to* TORRENCE)

I beg thee—beg thee!

TORRENCE (*flinging her aside*)

Away, thou slut! Thou bag of—who'll pluck this leech off me?

[DR. GRACE *and* MRS. MONTGOMERY *pull her back to the rear of the room.*

ROBINSON (*over his shoulder to* CARLOTTA)

Have no fear for me, pretty chick.

[CARLOTTA *glances up at the entrance door. There is someone's shadow upon it. She stands transfixed.*

CLEVELAND

Are you ready?

TORRENCE

Since yesterday, thick-skull!

CARLOTTA (*a sudden scream*)

Oh no! No! No!!

[*She turns away and covers her face.*

ROBINSON

Give us the count!

CLEVELAND (*counting slowly*)

One—two—three—four—five—six!

[TORRENCE *and* ROBINSON *advance a pace with each count as before, turn, and fire. Several shots are heard in rapid succession off Right. At the same instant a small jug on the shelf Down Left is shattered and falls to the floor.*

ROBINSON (*dropping his pistol*)

Stop! Stop! I—!

[*He staggers forward to the center of the stage.*

CARLOTTA (*rushing forward*)

Harry! Harry!

[CARLOTTA, DR. GRACE, MRS. MONTGOMERY, CLEVE-
LAND, *and* MRS. MAXWELL *surround* ROBINSON.

ROBINSON

I've been—! He's—! Wait, I'm—! (*With a sudden
deep groan.*) O-o-h!

[*He sways and falls back insensible. They lower him
to the stage in front of the table where he lies motionless in full view of the audience.* CARLOTTA *flings herself upon him.* CLEVELAND *stoops over the body.*

CLEVELAND (*as he examines the body*)

Clean through, east to— east to—

[*He suddenly stops and an expression of horror appears on his face. He takes his hand out of* ROBIN-
SON's *coat and holds it up. It is covered with blood.*
CARLOTTA *sees the blood and with a low moan turns
away and cowers upon the floor, her face in her
hands.*

DR. GRACE (*terribly agitated*)

For God's sake, Julian, what's happened?

CLEVELAND (*almost inaudibly*)

I—it looks like—

CARLOTTA

Oh no, no, *no!*

[MRS. MAXWELL *throws an agonized look at* DR. GRACE. TORRENCE *and* JESSUP, *who have been going through their business on the other side of the stage sense that something is wrong and are uncertain whether to continue the play or not.* MCAULIFFE *quickly and quietly goes out at Left. In the meantime, simultaneously with the foregoing speeches,* LANE *has entered and rushed down the steps.*

LANE

The Guard! The Guard! Did'st hear that volley? Jemmy! For thy life!

MCAULIFFE (*re-entering from Left*)

And don't move—any of you!
[*The curtain at the Rear falls quickly.*

MRS. MONTGOMERY

What's wrong? What's happened?

MCAULIFFE

Be quiet! Do you want to start a panic?

CLEVELAND

I'm afraid that Robinson's been shot.
[*Exclamations of horror.*

MCAULIFFE

That's why I rang down. We'll have to let the audience out. We can't go on with the show.

MRS. MONTGOMERY

But—!

MRS. MAXWELL

No, no! How *can* we go on with it?

MCAULIFFE

Somebody'd better go out and make an announcement.

CLEVELAND

I will.

MCAULIFFE

Don't let on that it's serious. Just tell 'em an accident's happened, and ask 'em to get out quickly.

CLEVELAND

Yes.

[*He goes up Back, and out through the center of the lowered curtain. There is applause from beyond the curtain.*

LANE

Better have a look at him, Dr. Grace.

DR. GRACE

What? Yes, yes! Of course!

[*He kneels beside* ROBINSON.

BRIGGS (*entering at right*)

What's happened?

MCAULIFFE

Robinson's been hurt. Send the crew away, and tell 'em to report at ten in the morning. Don't stop to ask questions!

[BRIGGS *opens his mouth to speak, then goes out quickly without a word. The others who have been watching* DR. GRACE *in tense silence, now turn their attention to* CLEVELAND, *whose voice begins to be heard off-stage behind the curtain.*

CLEVELAND (*from behind the curtain*)

Ladies and gentlemen, I regret to inform you that one of the members of the company has been suddenly taken ill. It is impossible to go on with the performance, and I must ask you to leave the theatre as quickly, and as quietly as possible. I thank you heartily for your co-operation, and wish you goodnight!

[DR. GRACE *replaces* ROBINSON'S *arm upon his breast.*

MRS. MAXWELL (*tensely*)

Well?

DR. GRACE

The worst, I'm afraid!

MRS. MAXWELL

What do you *mean?*

MCAULIFFE (*quietly*)

I thought so.

[CLEVELAND *re-enters through the curtain.*

CLEVELAND (*to* DR. GRACE)

Well, Edgar—? (DR. GRACE *looks up and shakes his head slowly.*) Are you *sure?*

[*The rear footlights and side-strips go out.*

DR. GRACE

Yes, quite sure. There's no pulse whatever, and there's a wound in his chest. I haven't examined it, but to have killed him instantly that way, the bullet must have gone straight through the heart. (*There is an awed silence as he rises.*) "Clean through—east to west—"

CARLOTTA

"He breathes, though." Remember? Oh, he *does* breathe?

DR. GRACE

No, my dear.
[*With a cry,* CARLOTTA *covers her face.*

MRS. MONTGOMERY

Oh, it's too terrible—too *terrible!*

MRS. MAXWELL

He can't be dead! How *could* he be dead? How could it have happened? Look again—you'll find he's just—

DR. GRACE

He's dead, Helen.

CLEVELAND

Quiet, everyone!
[JESSUP *leaves the curtain, and joins the group.*

MARIA (*entering hastily at Right*)

Mr. McAuliffe, the house-manager is here. He wants to know if—

CLEVELAND

Yes, I'll speak to him. (*As he goes to Right.*) Please do nothing till I come back.

MARIA

Is he—?

MCAULIFFE

Yes, Maria, he is.
[*The spot-lights on the stairs and the door go off.*

TORRENCE (*unable to restrain himself*)

Look here! I want to say—

DR. GRACE

Don't say anything until Mr. Cleveland gets back, Clarke.
[*A long silence.*

MRS. MONTGOMERY (*finally breaking the silence*)

Oh, I can't believe it!
[*The front X-rays and back spot-lights go off.*

DR. GRACE

Quiet, Alice!
[BRIGGS *enters. There is another silence, then* CLEVELAND *re-enters.*

JESSUP

Oughtn't we to send for the police?

CLEVELAND

I think that we can best find out exactly what happened without outside interference.

MR. MONTGOMERY

Oh yes! Yes, we must!

CLEVELAND

We shall have to be as cool and judicial as it is possible for us to be.

TORRENCE

That's all right—but *I'm* the one who's—

CLEVELAND

Quiet, please! Miss Scott, will you make sure that

everyone has left the theatre, and that all the doors are locked?

MARIA

Yes, sir.
[*She starts to go.*

CLEVELAND

Thank you.
[MARIA *goes out. Under the spell of* CLEVELAND's *authority, they all comply with his instructions.* JESSUP *and* MCAULIFFE *raise* CARLOTTA *from the floor and lead her to the Center of the stage.* LANE *brings a stool for her. The others group themselves in the Center at some distance from the body.*

JESSUP

I don't care what anybody says, I think we ought to send for the police.

BRIGGS

So do I.

LANE

Good Lord, yes!

CLEVELAND

There's time for that.

MCAULIFFE

It's the first thing to do.

JESSUP

Yes, Mr. Cleveland—

CLEVELAND

Just a moment! I know what police investigations are

like, and so do all of you. Before we subject ourselves to all that prying, and bungling, and scandal-
ous publicity, let us try to find out for ourselves how
this thing happened. (*An exclamation from all.*) I
am willing to take the responsibility for the delay on
my own shoulders, but I do *not* want to call in the
police until we have had an opportunity to conduct
an inquiry ourselves.

LANE

That makes sense, all right!

DR. GRACE

Yes—good sense.

CLEVELAND

Now, every one of us has just seen Robinson shot
to death before our eyes—possibly by accident, possibly with deliberate intent. We must find out which
—and it is in the interest of all of us, to arrive at
the truth as expeditiously as we can.

MRS. MONTGOMERY

It's too horrible! It really is!

CLEVELAND

I ask you all to co-operate with me—and above all,
I ask for absolute candor on the part of every one of
you. Is that agreed?
[*There is a silence.*

MCAULIFFE

Seems to be, doesn't it?

TORRENCE

Look here, I want to say—

CLEVELAND

I know, Torrence—there must be a good deal you want to say. But not yet please. Now let's see what the facts are. Robinson was killed by a bullet which entered his chest. We all observed, I take it, that at the moment of the shot, he uttered a cry of real pain?

TORRENCE

I thought at the time it was funny.

JESSUP

I didn't notice it.

BRIGGS

I did.

TORRENCE

So did I.

CLEVELAND

At any rate, we can assume that the jug that fell from the shelf above the bar was shattered by the ball which, in order to strike it, must have passed through his body.

MCAULIFFE (*pointing to the wall behind the bar*)

There's the hole it made.

TORRENCE

Where?

LANE

There. See?

JESSUP

Is it?

BRIGGS

I don't—oh yes!

CLEVELAND (*going around behind the bar*)

Yes, this is undoubtedly where the bullet passed through. (*Coming forward again.*) I'm afraid that all these circumstances indicate that the shot that killed Robinson was fired by Torrence. (*Murmurs of protest and incredulity.*) Wait, Torrence!

TORRENCE (*excitedly*)

I don't care what circumstances indicate what!

DR. GRACE

Look here, Julian, no one's going to stand up and shoot a man down before five hundred people.

TORRENCE

Not if he knows it, he isn't!

CLEVELAND

Please—! (*To* TORRENCE.) Your motives and intentions are another matter, to be considered separately. (*Unnoticed,* MARIA *enters at Back, coming through the curtain.*) The fact remains that you were standing opposite Robinson with a pistol in your hand, which you aimed and fired at him. Besides which, anyone else firing a shot would have been seen. (*To the* OTHERS.) Did any of you see anything which would lead you to believe that another person fired a shot? (*Silence.*) *Did* you?

JESSUP

  No.

DR. GRACE

  Not I. No.

MRS. MONTGOMERY

  Nor I.

BRIGGS

  I didn't see anything at all.

LANE

  Me, either.

TORRENCE

  I don't care what anybody says—

(together)

CLEVELAND (*directly at* CARLOTTA)

  So none of you saw anything which would admit of such a possibility?

MARIA

  Yes. (*They all turn in astonishment as she comes forward.*) I did.

MCAULIFFE (*to* MARIA)

  I thought you were back-stage.

MARIA

  I just went around front for a minute to see how the duel scene went.

MCAULIFFE

  Well, it didn't go so good.
[*The others glare at him.*

MRS. MONTGOMERY

Mr. McAuliffe, in the name of common decency—

MCAULIFFE

Beg pardon, Majesty. George's error. (*To* MARIA.) Is the audience out yet?

MARIA

Yes. Everyone has left the theatre, and I've locked all the doors.

CLEVELAND

Thank you. Now what did you see, Miss Scott? Please be as concise as you can.

MARIA (*pointing to the entrance door*)

Well, sir, that door there was opened just as Mr. Cleveland started counting, and before the shots were actually fired.

CLEVELAND

What of it? Oh—you infer from that, that the shot could have been fired from outside.

MARIA

It's only a suggestion.

CLEVELAND

Did any of the rest of you notice that?

MRS. MAXWELL

I didn't.

MRS. MONTGOMERY

Nor I! I doubt if anyone did! I doubt if it happened!

MCAULIFFE

If Maria saw it—it happened! She's the girl with the camera-eye. She kodaks, as she goes.

CLEVELAND

McAuliffe, you'll be good enough to—

LANE (*interrupting*)

As a matter of fact, the door did open. (*They all look at him.*) I know, because I opened it—and a moment or two ahead of time, in order not to be late on my cue.

MCAULIFFE

I told him to do that, so's not to hang up the scene. There was always a bad hole there.

CLEVELAND (*gravely*)

However, it does admit of another possibility.

LANE

Me, I suppose.

CLEVELAND

Yes.

MRS. MAXWELL

I've known Dickie Lane long enough to know that he's incapable of such a thing.

CARLOTTA

So have I! So have I!

LANE (*bitterly*)

Thanks. You're very kind!

CLEVELAND (*to* LANE)

You admit that you were standing just outside the partially open door, *before* the shots were fired?

LANE

Yes—what about it?

JESSUP (*bursting out*)

How could Dickie have done it? *He* didn't have any gun.

MARIA

Then why did Miss Maxwell look up toward the door and cry out—"Oh no! No! No!" That isn't in the script.
[*A pause.*

CLEVELAND (*gravely*)

You did do that, Carlotta?

CARLOTTA (*dully*)

Did I?

CLEVELAND

Yes. I remember now. You nearly cut Robinson's speech to me—"Give us the count."

CARLOTTA

I just—I just put it in—

CLEVELAND

No—*you* saw the door open, too. You saw Lane standing there.

MCAULIFFE

Don't pull any of this third-degree stuff, Cleveland, or somebody may ask *you* a question or two.

CLEVELAND

What do you mean?

MCAULIFFE

Nothing—nothing at all!

CLEVELAND

Anyone who wishes is at liberty to examine me.

MCAULIFFE

Thanks, I'll wait a bit.

CLEVELAND

Did you see Lane there, Carlotta?

CARLOTTA

No.

LANE

Yes you did.

CARLOTTA (*distractedly*)

I saw someone—

CLEVELAND

With something in his hand. Is that right?

CARLOTTA

I—I don't know what it was.

LANE

It was me, and I had a gun—two guns, I had—and I fired both of them.

MRS. MONTGOMERY

Dickie! You didn't!

LANE

I didn't kill him, no. If I'd wanted to kill the skunk, I'd have done it in the open.

MRS. MAXWELL

Be quiet, you foolish boy!

CLEVELAND

Please, Helen! (*To* LANE.) You don't improve your case by talking in that manner. We all know of your bitter feeling against Robinson.

LANE

Oh, don't be so damn pompous! What about yourself? Did you love him like a brother?

CARLOTTA (*half to herself*)

I don't believe Dickie killed him—no—

LANE

Thanks again!

CLEVELAND

Robinson told us that he was afraid you might attempt violence.

LANE

Oh, he did, did he?

CLEVELAND

That—plus the fact that you have been drinking—

LANE

*Am drunk,* please! I am drunk, you know.

CARLOTTA (*almost in a scream*)

Dickie! Don't talk like that!

LANE

> What do you care how I talk? (*To* CLEVELAND, *more calmly.*) I fired the two pistols off-stage, in the air. Hal asked me to help him, so as to get the shots right. Does that help you any, old Scotland Yard?

CLEVELAND

> Lane, I've nothing personal against you. You ought to realize that.

LANE

> All right—sorry. Examine away!

CLEVELAND

> Briggs—

BRIGGS (*nervously*)

> I found it hard to manage the script and all four guns, too, so I asked Dickie if he'd lend a hand.

CLEVELAND

> And fire two of the guns?

BRIGGS

> Yes. But—

CLEVELAND

> And did you see him fire them?

LANE

> I told you I fired them!

CLEVELAND (*to* BRIGGS)

> Did you see Lane fire the shots?

BRIGGS (*hesitating*)

> Well, I heard them go off.

CLEVELAND

But you actually didn't see in which direction they were fired.

BRIGGS (*angrily*)

Do you think you can make any of us believe—

CLEVELAND (*quietly*)

Did you?

BRIGGS (*confused*)

Well, I was back there under the light with the script, trying to get the timing right—(*Angrily.*) Mr. McAuliffe made such a row about the timing of that scene. *That's* why I asked Dickie to help.

CLEVELAND

Then no one saw the direction in which the pistols were fired. No one can testify that they were fired in the air.

LANE

Can anyone testify that they were fired at Robinson?

JESSUP

Yes—what about that?

CLEVELAND

We know that Dickie Lane had a grievance of some sort against Robinson—(LANE *exclaims impatiently.*) Just a moment, Lane! We know that he was on the scene at the time Robinson fell, we know that he had two pistols which he fired, we know that he is a perfect shot.

LANE

But, damn it to hell, I didn't do it!

CLEVELAND

I'm sorry, but there is a great deal to indicate that you did.

CARLOTTA

He couldn't have! I'm sure he couldn't!

CLEVELAND

Why are you sure?

CARLOTTA (*confused*)

I—I don't know. But I am!

MCAULIFFE

Just give me a word, will you? The shot that got Robinson was never fired by anyone standing six feet above the level of the stage. No matter how much one bird wanted to kill another, and no matter how good a shot he was, he couldn't make a bullet go through the body of somebody who was standing six feet below him, and have it go up again after it came out, and break a jug two feet over the man's head. I've known all the crack-shots in America for the last thirty years, but there isn't one of 'em could pull a stunt like that.
[*Murmurs of agreement.*

CLEVELAND

I believe you're right.

MCAULIFFE

I know I am!

CLEVELAND

It's a technical point which had not occurred to me.

MCAULIFFE

Technical point, my eye! It's a fact—and a fact that eliminates Lane completely, don't it?

CLEVELAND

Yes, I presume it does. In that event—

MARIA

In suggesting that you murdered him, I meant no offence, Mr. Lane.

LANE (*laughing shortly*)

That's quite all right.

TORRENCE (*to* CLEVELAND)

I think we should have kept the audience. Everyone out there was an eye-witness, do you realize that? They had the entire picture right before their eyes, as no one of us could possibly have it. The stage was brightly lighted, and there were only ten people on it—Robinson and nine others. If one of us nine killed Robinson, the one who did it must have been seen from out front.

MCAULIFFE (*cynically*)

Maybe!

MRS. MONTGOMERY

It was a subscription performance. We have a very complete list of everyone who was here.

TORRENCE

That doesn't help us now, though.

MARIA

*I* was in the audience.

MRS. MONTGOMERY

And did you see him killed?

MARIA

Yes.

LANE

"I," said the fly—

CARLOTTA

Don't, Dickie—don't!

TORRENCE

And who did it, Miss Scott?

MARIA

Well, I should say that you did.

MCAULIFFE

So would **I**.

TORRENCE (*to* CLEVELAND)

Listen! If that pistol had a bullet in it, I didn't know anything about it!

MCAULIFFE

Don't forget what he said this afternoon about having some kind of a grudge against Robinson.

TORRENCE (*indignantly*)

Robinson engineered a deal that very nearly ruined my father. Everybody knows about that. It was cause enough for a grudge—yes, a good grudge! But hardly for murder!

MCAULIFFE

I'm not saying out-and-out that you did it. I'm only saying that from your own story, it looks as though you might have been out to get him.

MRS. MONTGOMERY

Preposterous!
[*Murmurs of indignation from the others.*

CLEVELAND

I believe Mr. McAuliffe's point is legally sound. A motive in itself is not enough—but a motive coupled with other circumstances, may be.

DR. GRACE

Look here—is there any particular reason why the whole thing couldn't have been an accident?

CLEVELAND

It's difficult to see how.

DR. GRACE

Not at all. Somebody accidentally put a ball-cartridge into that particular gun, and unfortunately it was discharged at Robinson.

MRS. MONTGOMERY

Why, of course!

MRS. MAXWELL (*simultaneously*)

Yes, that's probably just what happened.

MCAULIFFE

Wouldn't that be sweet, though. "I didn't know it was loaded." (*They all look at him.*) Try and get away with it. Try to convince the police that bullets get into guns by accident.

CLEVELAND

Isn't it quite possible that there may have been one among the blank cartridges, and that it wasn't noticed?

MCAULIFFE

No, it isn't! The blanks come packed fifty in a box, and a ball-cartridge wouldn't fit in.

MARIA

Besides, I always examine them, so that—so that unnecessary blood may not be spilled.

TORRENCE

One! I didn't load that pistol—Two! It must have passed through several hands before it ever got into mine.

JESSUP

That's true enough, Mr. Cleveland.

CLEVELAND

Who did load the gun?

BRIGGS (*very nervously*)

I did. I loaded all of them, just as I was told to.

CLEVELAND

You would have known, wouldn't you, if one of the cartridges had had a bullet in it?

BRIGGS

Yes, of course I would. They were all blanks, I can swear to it.

CLEVELAND

Who else handled the guns after they were loaded?

BRIGGS

Well, there were—

MARIA

I examined them.

MCAULIFFE

And I brought them on stage.

TORRENCE

See? It's just as reasonable to assume that I accidentally shot Robinson with a gun that someone else had loaded, as it is to—

MRS. MONTGOMERY

It seems so to me, too.

JESSUP

I'm with you on that.

MCAULIFFE

Wait a minute! You can't get away with this, either. Maria and me are outsiders here, and it would suit you all a lot better if you could make it look like one of us did it, instead of one of your own crowd.

CLEVELAND

We are only trying to arrive at the truth, Mr. McAuliffe.

MCAULIFFE

All right! Then listen to me for a minute. Let's suppose that I, or Maria, or Briggs, was out to get Robinson.

BRIGGS (*protesting*)

I have always liked and admired Mr. Robinson.

MCAULIFFE (*ignoring him*)

And suppose one of us got the bright idea of planting a loaded gun on Torrence. How was the bird that cooked it up going to know that Torrence was going to pick out the right gun? And that once he did pick it out, he was going to shoot to kill?

CLEVELAND

Robinson is dead, is he not?

MCAULIFFE

One chance in a hundred. And one chance in four that he picked the right gun. Four hundred to one! That's a long chance for a guy to take, when he's out to kill somebody.

JESSUP

How do we know that all four guns weren't loaded?

LANE (*to* CLEVELAND)

There's a thought!

MRS. MONTGOMERY

Yes, Julian—perhaps you should look into that.

MCAULIFFE

Robinson's wasn't. If it was, something would have stopped the ball. And we can soon find out if the other two were. (*Gesturing towards the bar.*) There they sit—right there on the bar.

CLEVELAND

We'll examine them.

[*He goes and picks up the pistols.*

MCAULIFFE

But let's all see you do it!

CLEVELAND (*indignantly*)

That was my intention.
[*He approaches the group who come forward tensely as he opens the pistols, and removes the cartridges holding them up for inspection. It is seen that they are blanks.*

MCAULIFFE (*triumphantly*)

There you are! And now, while we're at it, let's look at the shell in Torrence's gun. (*Taking a pistol from the table.*) This it?

TORRENCE

Yes.
[MCAULIFFE *extracts the exploded shell from it, examines it, smiles, and passes shell and pistol to* CLEVELAND.

MCAULIFFE

It's a U. M. C.—what are the others?

CLEVELAND

DuPont.

MCAULIFFE

Also cast an eye at the neck of this shell—it's not crimped. They only crimp blanks. The crimping's to hold the wad in. You're some investigator, Mr. Cleveland. Those dumb police you despise so—they'd have found *that* out in the first two minutes.

LANE

How do *you* happen to know so much about it? *You're* not the police, are you?—Or *are* you?

MCAULIFFE

Not quite—but I'm a wise guy, when you really cut into me. And one more thing while I'm on the subject. If Maria, or Briggs, or me, did it—we'd be taking a chance that Robinson would pick the loaded gun and bump off Torrence. You'll have a hard time building a case out of that!

CLEVELAND (*angrily*)

I'm not trying to build a case, Mr. McAuliffe. I'm merely trying to get at the truth.

MRS. MONTGOMERY

It's a terrible, terrible thing that's happened. Let's not make it any worse by talking about murder. Somehow or other, a bullet got into that pistol—

MCAULIFFE (*sarcastically*)

Sure! Maybe it's a self-loader!

MRS. MONTGOMERY (*ignoring him*)

And Clarke, without having the slightest suspicion of it, accidentally killed Robinson.

MRS. MAXWELL

I quite agree.

DR. GRACE

Let's leave it at that.

BRIGGS

I—I feel sure it was an accident.

MCAULIFFE

It'd be nice, wouldn't it? Sure! For you it would. You're all good friends, and you don't like having your names in the paper. But me, I'm just a hard-boiled stage-director—a guy that don't appear to know very much—one of the birds that reads those newspapers. And when I see one bird that's good and sore at another stand up to him with a loaded gun and shoot him dead, you're going to have an awful time selling it to me as an accident!

TORRENCE (*angrily*)

Damn you, McAuliffe—

CLEVELAND

There's a great deal in what he says, Torrence. I am quite ready to accept it as an accident, but I don't see how we can delay any longer turning the case over to the police.

MRS. MONTGOMERY

But Good Heavens, Julian—they'd put Clarke in jail!

TORRENCE

You bet your neck they would.

CLEVELAND (*to* TORRENCE)

I think you can depend on most of us to support the accident theory. But, of course, there's no counting on how the circumstances will present themselves to the legal authorities.

DR. GRACE

Nor—nor on what the newspapers will make out of it, is there?

MARIA

And of course Mr. Torrence was present when Mr. McAuliffe explained how simple it would be to kill someone in the course of a play.
[*Angry exclamations against* MARIA.

CLEVELAND (*sharply*)

I think we can manage very well without your assistance!

MARIA

But, don't you remember? He said it was "a very useful piece of advice."

TORRENCE (*grinning*)

Miss Scott, I like you less and less.

MARIA

I'm sorry, Mr. Torrence, but you did say it.

CLEVELAND

I'm afraid there's nothing to do but telephone for the police. (*With a gesture to* BRIGGS.) Hal—do you mind?

BRIGGS (*decisively*)

Yes, I do!

CARLOTTA

And so do the rest of us!
[*The others murmur assent.*

TORRENCE

Thanks a lot, people.

MCAULIFFE (*sneering*)

Amateurs to the end! Well, I'll telephone! This is a
piece I'd like to see done by professionals.
[*He starts to move Right.*]

DR. GRACE

Just a moment.

MRS. MAXWELL (*alarmed*)

Edgar!

DR. GRACE (*continuing*)

Torrence is entirely innocent.

CLEVELAND

How do you know that?

DR. GRACE

Because it was I who put the bullet in the gun.
[MRS. MONTGOMERY *gasps.*

CARLOTTA (*moaning*)
  Oh—!                    } (together)
TORRENCE
  What the—?

MRS. MAXWELL

You didn't! You did nothing of the sort!

CLEVELAND

What are you saying, Edgar?

DR. GRACE

That I put the bullet in the gun.

CLEVELAND

But, why on earth—?

DR. GRACE

I had a very strong personal motive for wanting to prevent Robinson from sailing tonight. The possibility of injuring him in the course of the duel scene, without being detected, occurred to me.
[*There is general surprise and dismay.*

CARLOTTA

Oh, Uncle Ned—

DR. GRACE

"Injuring," I said. I never intended to kill him. It was my intention to wound him with my dagger, so that he wouldn't be able to sail.

MRS. MONTGOMERY

Dagger? But he was *shot*, Edgar!

DR. GRACE

Please wait a moment, Alice. (*To* CLEVELAND.) Then I realized what a cowardly thing it would be to stab a man in the back. So I determined to face him—tell him just what I was going to do—do it, and take the consequences. I concluded that a pistol would be less unpleasant than a knife. So I went to buy one. I found they don't sell them without a permit. Then I remembered that these pistols we use in the play, were made for modern cartridges. Hal kept them in my dressing-room—

CLEVELAND

You mean, in the course of the scene you intended—

DR. GRACE

No. I intended to do it in his dressing-room, when the play was over.

CLEVELAND

But then, how did—?

DR. GRACE

So I bought some cartridges, and came to the theatre early. Four of the eight pistols were there on my table, loaded with blanks. I found a sized-cartridge that fitted one of the guns perfectly. I had barely slipped it into the breech, when Hal came in, without knocking.

BRIGGS

I didn't know you were there yet.

DR. GRACE

I was merely explaining why I hadn't had time to get it out again. He said, "I've got to have those pistols for the off-stage shots."

CLEVELAND (*to* BRIGGS)

Did you say that?

BRIGGS

Yes—that's exactly what I said.

DR. GRACE

Then I said, "What about the ones Torrence and Robinson use?" And he said—

CLEVELAND

Yes, Briggs—?

BRIGGS

I said, "Oh, I've already got those in place." And he laughed and said, "You didn't forget to load them, did you?" And I laughed and said, "You bet I didn't. Not this time!"

DR. GRACE

So I let him take the four for the off-stage shots.

CLEVELAND

Including the one with the bullet?

DR. GRACE

Yes.

CLEVELAND

Without removing it?

DR. GRACE

Yes. I thought I'd have time to get it before the curtain went up, but something intervened, and I hadn't. It worried me of course, but I told myself that Hal always fired the off-stage shots in the air—I'd seen him rehearse it—and that the chance of the bullet doing any damage was quite negligible.

CLEVELAND

Just a minute, Edgar. We are to understand that later you intended to reload that same pistol and shoot Robinson with it?

DR. GRACE

That had been my intention, yes.

CLEVELAND

"Had been—?"

DR. GRACE

Before the curtain ever went up, I learned something that made me change my mind entirely.

CLEVELAND

Indeed.

DR. GRACE

*Entirely!* Before I set foot on this stage tonight, I had entirely given up my plan to injure him.

CLEVELAND

What had you learned?

DR. GRACE

I can't tell you that. It can only say that it was something that convinced me that it was no longer necessary to prevent his sailing.

MCAULIFFE

Well, *that's* one of the nicest, thinnest stories ever I heard.

DR. GRACE

You can keep out of this, McAuliffe!

CLEVELAND

He's right, though. If your change of mind is to have any practical bearing, we must know what caused the change.

DR. GRACE (*quietly*)

Well, you're not going to, Julian.

MRS. MAXWELL

Edgar—I—

DR. GRACE

Please Helen—don't interfere. (*To* CLEVELAND.) I think just now you'd do better to find out how the loaded gun that Hal took for the off-stage shots, happened to get among those used in the duel. Don't you?

BRIGGS

That's what *I'd* like to know. I had them—

MARIA (*interrupting*)

I think perhaps I can explain that point.

CLEVELAND (*turning on her*)

Oh? *How* can you?

MARIA

When I examined the pistols, I noticed that one of the four that had been put aside for the duel was different than the one we ordinarily used in that scene. So I looked among the others, and finding the right one there *I* made the exchange.

MCAULIFFE

Leave it to Maria to get things right.

MRS. MONTGOMERY

You see, Miss Scott, what comes of your meddling.

MARIA

I'm very sorry, Mrs. Montgomery, but of course I was unaware of Dr. Grace's intention to shoot Mr. Robinson.

DR. GRACE

I am entirely innocent. I never wanted to kill him, and the substitution of the pistols no one could possibly have foreseen.

[MCAULIFFE *draws a deep, impatient breath.*

LANE

Robinson might have picked the wrong gun, himself.

MRS. MONTGOMERY

Well, that clears everything up, Julian. It was an accident, just as I said all along.

CLEVELAND

I'm afraid it isn't as simple as that. Robinson is dead —shot by the pistol which Edgar loaded. Is that "death from accidental causes"? Is it?

DR. GRACE

Yes!

CLEVELAND

You say you changed your mind. Why did you change your mind? And what was your reason for wanting to injure Robinson in the first place?

DR. GRACE

I can't tell you that! And I don't see what difference it makes?

CLEVELAND (*gravely*)

It makes a great deal of difference, Edgar. You acknowledge you made preparations to shoot a man. As a direct result of your preparations, the man is killed. And for your alleged "change of mind," you refuse to divulge either motive or reason. Don't you see how badly it looks?

MCAULIFFE

Just bad enough to send him up for twenty years or so—that's all!

MRS. MAXWELL

It was my—

DR. GRACE (*to* CLEVELAND)

I'll have to take my chances, then!

MCAULIFFE

Twenty years, if he's lucky.—If he isn't—

CARLOTTA (*suddenly*)

I'll tell you why he wanted to do it—why he decided *not* to do it! I had planned to sail tonight on the *Berengaria,* too—
[*Murmurs of surprise from the others.*

CLEVELAND

You mean, you and Robinson?

CARLOTTA

Yes.

CLEVELAND

Carlotta, were you planning an elopement with Robinson?

CARLOTTA

We were both going to Paris, that's all. He was to get his divorce, and then we were to be married.

CLEVELAND

Divorce! He told you he was going to get a divorce?

CARLOTTA

Yes, of course he did.

CLEVELAND

But I know it to be a fact that my sister had absolutely refused to give him a divorce. And he knew it too. He knew that nothing would change her.

MRS. MAXWELL

You see, Carlotta—!

LANE

Oh, the rotten—!

JESSUP

Go easy, Dickie.

CARLOTTA

He told me that it was all arranged, and I believed him. Mother found out about what I was planning to do, and she and my Uncle tried to persuade me not to go. But I was determined to go anyhow. I never dreamt that—(*Turning to* DR. GRACE.) What made you think of anything so mad?

CLEVELAND (*to* CARLOTTA)

Please finish what you were saying?

CARLOTTA (*continuing*)

This evening before the performance, I wanted to see him. I knocked on the door of his dressing-room and went in. He wasn't there. I was going to go out again, when I saw some letters on the make-up table.

One of them was postmarked Paris, and was in a woman's handwriting. I suppose it was a contemptible thing for me to do, but I had heard so many stories, and—well, anyhow, whether I had a right to or not, I read the letter.

[*She stops, overcome by emotion.*

CLEVELAND

Yes?

CARLOTTA (*continuing*)

It was from a girl in Paris. She said she was writing from her death-bed. She accused him of getting her to go to Paris with him, by promising to marry her there—then of treating her shamefully, and deserting her. She said that he was responsible for her death. I can't tell you how awful it was—full of curses, and all sorts of terrible things.

[*She begins to sob.*

LANE (*going to her*)

Carlotta, my dear.

CARLOTTA (*pushing him away*)

I'm all right now. (*To* CLEVELAND.) I put the letter back and went out of the dressing-room. On my way back to my own dressing-room, I stopped at my Uncle's and told him he needn't worry any more— that I had changed my mind, that I wasn't going.

CLEVELAND

Did you tell him why?

CARLOTTA

No, I didn't. He asked me—but I couldn't talk about it.

CLEVELAND (*to* DR. GRACE)

It was when Carlotta told you that she didn't intend to go with Robinson, that you gave up your plan to attack him?

DR. GRACE

Yes. If Carlotta was staying, I was only too glad to have him go. I should have unloaded the gun, of course, but—well, I didn't. It never occurred to me that anyone would be hurt by it.

CLEVELAND

And what are we going to tell the authorities?

DR. GRACE

That it was an accident.

CLEVELAND

I'm afraid it will mean divulging the whole story. I see no way of keeping Carlotta's name out of it.

LANE

Carlotta hasn't done anything she need be ashamed of. The only person who'll be disgraced is that damned rat, who got what he deserved!

JESSUP

Right! (*To* CLEVELAND.) Shall I telephone now, Mr. Cleveland?

CLEVELAND

Will you?

[JESSUP *starts to move Right, to go out.*

MARIA (*who has been waiting for a chance to speak.*

There's just one little point that still bothers me.

(JESSUP *stops*.) I've been thinking about what Mr. McAuliffe said. It seems very strange to me that Mr. Torrence, who isn't a marksman—no? And who is constantly complaining about his eyes—it seems very remarkable that he should have aimed the pistol so accurately, that the bullet killed Mr. Robinson at once.

DR. GRACE

I assure you that he was dead when I lifted his hand—

CLEVELAND

He was dead before that—he was dead when I bent over him.

JESSUP

Still, if he died from some other cause—some disease or other, apoplexy, say—then there couldn't be any talk about murder, could there?

CLEVELAND

It isn't likely that he did.

LANE

Nor is it likely that Clarke shot as straight as that.

DR. GRACE

Of course, I *didn't* examine the wound. I was terribly agitated, and it seemed obvious that—(*Before anyone can stop him, he goes quickly to* ROBINSON's *body and kneels beside it. Several of the other men crowd around him as he open* ROBINSON's *clothing. He exposes the wound.*) See here!

LANE

That bullet never could have killed him!

DR. GRACE

You're right! It's made nothing more than a super-
ficial wound—passed through the fleshy part of his
shoulder, that's all.
[*Exclamations of astonishment.*

CLEVELAND

Then we must have a thorough examination imme-
diately, to determine the exact cause of his death.

DR. GRACE

I think someone other than me had better make it,
don't you?

CLEVELAND

I'll call Dr. Edwards, shall I?

DR. GRACE

Yes, do.

JESSUP

Suppose we get the body out of here into one of the
dressing-rooms?

LANE

Good idea!

MRS. MONTGOMERY

Oh yes, by all means!

CLEVELAND

We shouldn't move that body!

DR. GRACE

It's impossible to make an adequate examination here.

LANE

Couldn't we mark the exact position on the floor?

CLEVELAND (*hesitatingly*)

Well, I suppose since we can all testify that—

LANE (*quickly*)

Let's then! Where's that chalk of yours, Miss Scott?

MARIA

Here.
[*She hands him the chalk, and he outlines on the stage
the position of the body.*

LANE (*as he finishes*)

There you are!

JESSUP

Give me a hand, some of you, will you? (*A cloak is
thrown over the body, and* JESSUP *and* CLEVELAND
*take* ROBINSON *under the shoulders, while* BRIGGS *and*
TORRENCE *take him by the feet.*) All right, now!
[*They raise the body from the floor, and as they do
so, a knife clatters to the floor. The* WOMEN *scream
and the* MEN *recoil in astonishment.*

CARLOTTA (*with a scream*)

Look! His back! A dagger!!

CLEVELAND

Turn him over!
[*They turn* ROBINSON'S *body over and lower it face*

*downwards to the stage.* MCAULIFFE *comes around and bends over the body.*

MCAULIFFE

Stabbed to the heart, through the back! Lord Almighty!!

[CLEVELAND *rises, turns, and looks penetratingly at* DR. GRACE.

DR. GRACE

What's the matter, Julian?

CLEVELAND

So you didn't change your mind about the dagger!

MRS. MAXWELL

No! No!! Wait! Please wait! I want to—

[*She gropes for the table, tries to steady herself, and slumps into a chair, unable to speak.*

CURTAIN

# ACT THREE

# ACT THREE

*Scene: The same setting as Act II.*

*The table at Left has been moved a little up-stage so that it stands over the knife on the floor, to prevent its being moved.* ROBINSON's *gloves on the bar have the fingers pointing in opposite directions.* ROBINSON's *body has been removed. In all other respects the scene is identical with the end of the preceding Act.*

*Time: The time is a few minutes after the conclusion of Act II.*

*At Rise: The lights, and the lighting of the room are also the same as the end of Act II and the same characters are discovered:* CARLOTTA, MRS. MONTGOMERY, LANE, *and* DR. GRACE *are grouped about* MRS. MAXWELL, *who is seated in a chair, Center.*

MRS. MAXWELL (*her voice heard before the curtain rises*)

Julian, listen to me.—(*The Curtain rises.*) Edgar is entirely innocent, do you understand? You mustn't think of accusing him. He didn't do it—he knows nothing about it!

MCAULIFFE

How do you happen to be sure of that?

MRS. MAXWELL

Because I know who did do it! (*Exclamations of surprise.*) I think when a person kills a man, she—she—

129

CLEVELAND

Steady, Helen!

MCAULIFFE (*approaching* CLEVELAND)

Why "steady"?

CLEVELAND

Of course, if you really know, it is your duty to tell us.

MRS. MAXWELL

I'm going to tell you. I did it, myself!

CARLOTTA

Mother!

DR. GRACE

It's not true!

MRS. MONTGOMERY

Helen, how could you?                    } (together)

LANE

Rot! I don't believe it!

CLEVELAND

Do you know what you're saying, Helen?

MRS. MAXWELL

Yes, I do!

DR. GRACE

She's talking nonsense! You can see how overwrought she is!

CLEVELAND

Don't complicate this by any silly false admissions.

That won't help Edgar—it won't help anyone.

**MCAULIFFE**

Seems to me she ought to know whether she did or not.

**DR. GRACE** (*seizing* CLEVELAND's *arm*)

You mustn't believe her, Julian. She's trying to protect *me*, that's all.

**CLEVELAND**

You admit *you* did it, then?

**DR. GRACE**

No! No! I've *told* you my story. I'm entirely innocent.

**MCAULIFFE**

Then what's all this for? Eh? How about it?

**DR. GRACE**

Mrs. Maxwell knew what I intended to do. And now, because suspicion has centered on me—(*Turning to* MRS. MAXWELL.) Helen, I swear to you I know nothing of this—nothing!

**CARLOTTA** (*shaking* MRS. MAXWELL)

Mother! Why are you so foolish? You know you couldn't possibly have done it!

**MRS. MAXWELL** (*brokenly*)

I—no—you're right, I couldn't have—

**MCAULIFFE** (*disgustedly*)

Lord Almighty!

DR. GRACE

Listen to me. Helen could have had no possible motive for this crime. I told her before the performance began that Carlotta was not going with Robinson.

CLEVELAND

You did?

DR. GRACE

Yes.

MCAULIFFE

That's what *you* say! Did anybody hear you?

DR. GRACE

Look here, McAuliffe—!

MCAULIFFE

No! *You* look! (*He turns to the* OTHERS.) Ladies and gentlemen here assembled, I know you're very good friends, real buddies, and all that—but this is a pretty serious business. A man has been murdered —stabbed in the back—and if you ask me, it's time we stopped being so god-damn polite about it—

MRS. MONTGOMERY

Mr. McAuliffe! *Please*—

MCAULIFFE (*paying no attention to her*)

—And get down to cases!

CLEVELAND

Suppose you let me manage it, McAuliffe.

MCAULIFFE

Suppose I don't! That's just what I'm getting at.

You don't quite qualify for the judgment-seat, no!
Nor for all this criss-cross-examination, either. Because if there's one thing here that's dead certain, it's
that one of the five people that was around Robinson when he fell, put that knife in his back!

MRS. MONTGOMERY

You don't mean to include *me*, I hope!

MCAULIFFE (*sharply*)

Yes, Madam, I do! (*Pointing in turn to* DR. GRACE,
MRS. MAXWELL, CARLOTTA, *and* CLEVELAND.) And you
—and you—and you—*and you!*

CLEVELAND

Well?

MCAULIFFE

Yes, "well"! Back in the sticks, where I come from,
they don't let the investigation be done by one of
the birdies under suspicion. It ain't cricket!

MRS. MONTGOMERY

And will you kindly tell me why *I* should be under
suspicion?

MCAULIFFE

You got two hands, and a funny manner—that's
why! (*To* CLEVELAND.) How about it?

CLEVELAND

Very well. We shall let Torrence take the investigation in hand.

TORRENCE

Not for me, thanks. *I'm* not going to say another
word.

MCAULIFFE

It's time the police took it in hand, if you ask me!

DR. GRACE

No—not yet!

MRS. MAXWELL

No—please—please!  (together)

MRS. MONTGOMERY

Not the police! No—we mustn't!

MCAULIFFE

Maria, call the police!

MARIA

Yes, sir.

[*She starts to go out.* CLEVELAND *intercepts her.*

CLEVELAND

No, we don't want the police.

MCAULIFFE

You particularly, eh? Just a little leary of a real investigation, eh?

CLEVELAND

You think I—(*Suddenly.*) Very well. Send for them!

MRS. MONTGOMERY

And then we'll all be locked up—all of us!

MCAULIFFE

Oh, I guess not—I guess we'll run down the guy who did it, before they get here—or the dame who did it! Go along, Maria! (MARIA *goes out.*) Now, what have we got? (*Counting off on his fingers.*) We've got

Grace here, admitting that he was out to get Robinson—

DR. GRACE

I have told you my entire story. It stands as I told it.

MCAULIFFE

Sure—I know—you changed your mind! Then, we've got Mrs. Maxwell confessing that *she* did it—

MRS. MAXWELL

No, no!

MCAULIFFE

But she's changed *her* mind!

LANE

Look here, McAuliffe—!

MCAULIFFE (*wearily*)

Honest, if anyone else says "Look here!" to me, my eyes are liable to pop right out at 'em.

CLEVELAND

Go ahead.

MCAULIFFE

—And we've got Mrs. Montgomery, who seems to be a whole lot more nervous than what you'd expect of an innocent bystander—

MRS. MONTGOMERY

I? Nervous? How absurd! (*She laughs hysterically.*) What have I to fear?

MCAULIFFE

Oh, the pen—or the electric chair—I dunno. Then

here's little Miss Maxwell, who I guess didn't feel any
too friendly towards our friend Robinson after reading about Mary Clinton.

CARLOTTA

However I may have felt, I never—
[*Her voice breaks.*

LANE

Be careful whom you accuse, McAuliffe!

MCAULIFFE

Keep cool, kid. When it comes to murder, your girl's
no better than anybody else.

CARLOTTA
Dickie!

CLEVELAND (*interrupting*)
Who's Mary Clinton?

MCAULIFFE

Isn't she the girl who wrote that letter? Didn't you
hear Miss Maxwell say so?

JESSUP
I don't remember.

LANE
No, I didn't.

MCAULIFFE

Well, she did—whether you heard her or not! That
shows what testimony is worth. (*To* MARIA *as she re-
enters.*) Did you get them?

MARIA
Yes, sir. They'll hurry right over.

MCAULIFFE

Did you say what'd happened?

MARIA

No, I didn't want to alarm them.—It's late.

LANE

What the—!
[TORRENCE *laughs.*

MARIA

I mean, I thought you'd all prefer it if they didn't
send the patrol.

TORRENCE

Score one for Miss Scott!

MARIA

They're coming though. I said it was rather urgent.

MCAULIFFE

You should have said murder!

LANE

Keep going, McAuliffe. You've checked off four, now.
Who's the fifth?

MCAULIFFE

For number five, we've got Mr. Cleveland, who wasn't
exactly pally with the deceased I guess, in spite of
being partners and all.

DR. GRACE

You're bent upon involving every one of us, aren't
you?

MCAULIFFE

I'm just trying to show how things look when **you** quit making courtesies at 'em! (*He turns to* CLEVELAND.) Cleveland, you and Robinson had a run-in this afternoon in Robinson's dressing-room. I could hear you away back in the prop-room. And I guess I wasn't the only one with an ear cocked! (*Turning to the* OTHERS.) Was I? Eh? *Was* I?

BRIGGS (*after a hesitating pause*)

As a matter of fact, *I* heard some kind of rumpus.

LANE

So did **I**.

TORRENCE

Dickie and **I** both did.

CLEVELAND

I have nothing to conceal about it. I did have a quarrel with Robinson. His wife is my sister, and I had reason to object to his treatment of her. And I told him so!

MCAULIFFE

In so many words?

CLEVELAND

In so many words!

MCAULIFFE

Among 'em being, "I'm going to put an end to this"?

DR. GRACE

Did you say that, Julian?

CLEVELAND

I believe I did. But it's scarcely a basis for a murder charge.

MCAULIFFE

We'll see if it is. Well, Jessup—this leaves you and Briggs and Maria and me, as the only ones at which the well-known finger of suspicion does not point. So most likely it was one of us, did it.

LANE

It wouldn't be a bad idea to find out whose knife that is, on the floor.

MCAULIFFE

You're right, it wouldn't!

DR. GRACE

Here's my knife.

CLEVELAND

And mine.

JESSUP

And here's mine.

TORRENCE

Mine, too.

MCAULIFFE

Proves nothing! Neither Cleveland nor Grace would be fool enough to use his own knife. (*To* MARIA.) Is it one of the prop knives, Maria?

MARIA

No. None of them has a polished handle like that one.

TORRENCE (*bending down closely over the knife on the floor*)

Wait a minute! I've got a hunch.

MCAULIFFE (*quickly*)

Don't touch that knife!

TORRENCE

I'm not touching it. I'm trying to see if there are any finger-prints.

LANE

You can't without a glass, can you?

BRIGGS

On a surface like that you ought to be able to. It's polished brass.

TORRENCE

The queer part of it is, there don't seem to be any— prints, I mean.

DR. GRACE

Of course there are finger-prints. There must be!

MCAULIFFE

Yeah? Why?

JESSUP (*going to the knife*)

Your eyes are bum, Clarke. Give me a look. (*He examines the knife.*) Looks smooth as glass to me. (*To* BRIGGS.) Try it, Hal.

BRIGGS (*examining the knife*)

Nope! You're right.

LANE

If there were prints there, we'd see them.

MCAULIFFE

Give me a squint, will you? (*He looks.*) No—not a mark.

LANE (*looking closely at the knife*)

There isn't so much as a touch on it.

MCAULIFFE

Maria, come here a minute, and turn one of your lenses on this one.

MARIA (*she goes over swiftly, and takes one brief look at the knife*)

There are no finger-prints on that handle!

MCAULIFFE

Well, that shows that whoever did it, had sense enough to wrap it in something—a sleeve or a handkerchief, maybe.

MARIA (*suddenly*)

I have it!

[*Everyone starts nervously at this cry.*

CLEVELAND

What is it, Miss Scott?

MARIA (*pointing dramatically*)

Mrs. Montgomery—

MRS. MONTGOMERY

Oh! Oh! I knew this was coming—I've been waiting for this! (*Hysterically.*) It's not true! It's not true!

MARIA

I've reconstructed it all, as I saw it! Just before Mr. Robinson fell, Mrs. Montgomery raised her arm—like this—

[*She illustrates with her left arm.*

MRS. MONTGOMERY

I didn't! I never did!

MARIA

But I saw you!

CLEVELAND

Did you see anything in her hand?

MARIA

No, I couldn't have. It was too quick—like that—(*She illustrates again.*) And I've noticed before that Mrs. Montgomery is left-handed.

MRS. MONTGOMERY

That isn't so!

CLEVELAND

Be careful, Alice—we all know that you're left-handed. Only yesterday, you said—

MRS. MONTGOMERY

Well, what if I am?

CLEVELAND

If you can satisfactorily explain your gesture—

MRS. MONTGOMERY

It's all this terrible woman! Why did we ever tolerate such a person?

CLEVELAND

Do you know anything about this murder, Alice?

MRS. MONTGOMERY

Of course I don't! It's a lie—a downright lie! She's just a presumptuous, dowdy, meddlesome, little busybody!

MARIA

I'm sure that character counts for as much as wealth and fine clothes, Mrs. Montgomery. Were you in love with Mr. Robinson?

MRS. MONTGOMERY (*to* CLEVELAND)

Julian, you're my lawyer! Are you going to let that impossible creature accuse me of such things?

CLEVELAND

You'd do much better to be calm, Alice.

MARIA

What I accused you of, was of raising your arm.

MRS. MONTGOMERY

I didn't raise my arm!

MARIA

I saw you!

MRS. MONTGOMERY (*suddenly remembering*)

Oh!

CLEVELAND

What is it?

MRS. MONTGOMERY

Wait, I'm trying to remember. While we were all

there, around Robin, I remember feeling something catch at my sleeve—just for an instant.

CLEVELAND

You mean, you *may* have raised your arm?

MRS. MONTGOMERY

Yes, I'm sure now, that I did. I felt the thing, whatever it was, and without thinking—
[*She raises her left arm.*

JESSUP

Look! The sleeve is all torn!

MRS. MONTGOMERY

Where?

LANE (*examining the sleeve*)

It's a long, clean slit! Must have been something sharp, all right.

BRIGGS

It wasn't like that when you put it on, was it?

MRS. MONTGOMERY

No. Of course not.

CLEVELAND

You think it happened just at that moment?

MRS. MONTGOMERY

It must have. I remember feeling something for just that second. Then everything happened at once, and I forgot all about it.

TORRENCE (*grinning*)

But Miss Scott didn't. Not Miss Scott!

JESSUP

It was the dagger, I guess. In close quarters, like that, it could easily have happened.

MCAULIFFE

It may have been just a pin, or something on somebody's costume.

LANE

A pin'd have a hard time making a six-inch slit in a piece of heavy cotton.

CLEVELAND

But if it was done by the knife that was plunged into Robinson, we cannot suspect Alice. She couldn't have slit her own sleeve at the moment of stabbing Robinson.

MRS. MONTGOMERY (*happily*)

I couldn't, could I?

LANE

Then, who did? After all—there it is!

MARIA

If you're willing to walk through the scene again, perhaps I can tell you who did.
[*Murmurs of dissent from the* OTHERS.

JESSUP

I think all we can do now, is wait for the police.

CLEVELAND

I'm more than willing that Miss Scott should—

LANE

So am I.

TORRENCE

But, if she didn't see anything in the first place—

MARIA

—But the positions may refresh my memory.

MRS. MONTGOMERY

Good Heavens—how can we be expected to do any acting, when we're all faced with prison?

MARIA

It will only mean walking through the positions.

MCAULIFFE

No more than you usually do!

JESSUP

I don't see the harm in trying it.

TORRENCE

All right. Let's do it, then.

DR. GRACE

Yes.

BRIGGS

We'd better hurry, don't you think? It was some time ago that Miss Scott telephoned for the police.

MRS. MONTGOMERY

If she ever did!

MARIA

There is no doubt about it, Mrs. Montgomery. I distinctly remember telephoning. (*She turns to the* OTHERS.) Now then, let's begin at the point at which the pistols are chosen. Will you all find your places please? And Mr. Briggs, will you take the part Mr. Robinson played?

BRIGGS

Yes, I guess I can. Where's that script?
[JESSUP *takes the script from the table and hands it to him.*

MARIA (*standing down-stage Center, her back to the footlights*)

Now, if you'll all—let's see—you're off-stage, Mr. Lane.

LANE

You want my entrance?

MARIA

Just from the foot of the steps, I think.
[LANE *goes to the foot of the steps.*

MCAULIFFE (*behind the bar*)

You'll never get it right, with someone else in the most important part!

TORRENCE

Well, unfortunately, we can't have Robinson play it.

MARIA (*suddenly and excitedly*)

One of those gloves on the bar—!

MCAULIFFE (*interrupting quickly. Pointing to the open door at the top of the steps opposite*)

Who's that up there?

[*Involuntarily, everyone, including* MARIA, *looks up at the door,* LANE *leaps up the steps, and out through the door.* MCAULIFFE'S *hands swiftly glided over the gloves, and then he moves several feet away up-stage.*

JESSUP

   Where?

DR. GRACE

   What?

TORRENCE                                           (together)

   What is it?

MRS. MAXWELL

   Don't! Don't! I can't stand it!

LANE (*his voice heard off-stage outside the door*)

   Anybody there?

MCAULIFFE

   I swear I thought I saw that door swing back, and someone move behind it.

LANE (*coming back inside the room*)

   There's no one here.

CLEVELAND

   Are you sure?

LANE

   Not a soul!

MCAULIFFE

   The cops, maybe—
   (LANE *descends the steps slowly, watching* MCAULIFFE.)

Lord! I guess this thing's got *me* going, even. Sorry, folks.

MRS. MONTGOMERY

I shan't sleep for weeks—I know I shan't.

TORRENCE

Well, shall we play the scene?

MARIA

One moment. I don't understand about those gloves—
(*She moves toward the bar, then stops in astonishment.*) Why!

DR. GRACE

What's wrong?

MARIA

I don't understand this at all. Just a moment ago, I was sure that—
[*She stops, staring in bewilderment at the gloves.*

CLEVELAND

Sure about what?

MARIA (*after a moment's pause*)

Never mind, we'll wait—we'll come back to it. (*She turns from the gloves.*) Now then, Mr. Briggs, you and Mr. Torrence are at the bar—choosing the pistols. The others around them. (*As the* OTHERS *take their places.*) A little further up-stage, Mr. Briggs. That's it. And Mrs. Montgomery, you're back just a little more. No, that's too much! That's right. Now, all hold that for just a moment, please. Oh, and will you put on the gloves, so that we get that right? (BRIGGS *puts on the gloves.* MARIA *stands watching them all.*) Now if you'll begin, Mr. Briggs—"Will you choose?"

BRIGGS (*searching the script for the place*)

Wait a minute. Oh yes, here it is. (*Reading from the script.*) "Will you choose?"

TORRENCE

"After you, m'lord." (*To* MARIA.) Look here, are we going to use the guns?

CLEVELAND

Better not, I think.

MARIA

It won't be necessary, if you'll just indicate the business—

MCAULIFFE

You seem kind of nervous, Maria—bad trait in a stage-director.

MARIA

It's my first experience, Mr. McAuliffe. (*To* BRIGGS.) Go on please, Mr. Briggs. "I'm a commoner like yourself—"

BRIGGS (*reading*)

"I'm a commoner like yourself, do you undertsand?"

TORRENCE

"Yes, m'lord—or more so."

MARIA

Laughter! —Now, business of picking out pistol, Mr.

Briggs. That's it. And you weren't quite so close, Mr. Cleveland.

CLEVELAND

I always stood right here.

MARIA

In rehearsal, yes. But not at the performance to-night. This is tonight's performance.

CLEVELAND (*moving away a little*)

Here, then?

MARIA

Yes, that's it. All right Mr. Briggs, you have the pistol now.

BRIGGS

Yes. Business. Now I turn away. "This will do me." [*Turning away.*

MARIA

Yes. Not quite so far, though. There!

TORRENCE

That's me, isn't it? Pick up pistol. "So will this." Laughter. Turn. "Spread out, you—"

MARIA

No—wait a moment!

TORRENCE

Oh yes—I forgot that line, didn't I? (*To* MCAULIFFE.) And you jumped in and saved me.

MCAULIFFE

I expected you'd slip up somewhere, so I was ready.

What did I say, Maria? I forget—something about elbow-room—

MARIA

You said—"Give the lad a little elbow-room."

MCAULIFFE

"Give the lad a little elbow-room."

[DR. GRACE, MRS. MONTGOMERY, *and* JESSUP *go upstage.* CLEVELAND *and* MRS. MAXWELL *remain downstage.*

MARIA

You brushed against Mr. Robinson as you went up, Mrs. Montgomery.

MRS. MONTGOMERY (*indignantly*)

Brushed against him! Certainly not! Why should I brush against him?

MARIA

I don't know. But you did. This way—
[*She illustrates by going Down and Up again, brushing against* BRIGGS *as she passes him.*

MRS. MONTGOMERY

I did nothing of the kind!

MARIA

I beg your pardon. I distinctly remember it.

MRS. MONTGOMERY

I tell you—

MARIA (*with sudden sharpness*)

Will you please be quiet, and do as I say?

CLEVELAND

Don't argue, Alice, and let's get on.

MRS. MONTGOMERY

She'll be saying next, that she saw me stab him.

MARIA

Perhaps I shall. If I did see you, I shall.

TORRENCE

Say, listen—!

DR. GRACE                } (together)

Really, Miss Scott—

MARIA (*sharply*)

Quiet! Damn it, will you do as I say, everyone! How often must I tell you!
[*There is a stunned silence.*

CLEVELAND

Am I next? Yes. "It is agreed between you. Six paces, turn, and fire."

TORRENCE

"Agreed!"
[*He strides to the middle of the stage.*

BRIGGS

Now what do I do?

MARIA

You take your gloves off and throw them on the floor.

BRIGGS

Like this?
[*He throws one glove on the floor.*

MARIA

Yes. Mr. Robinson evidently forgot at first. Now pick it up, and put it on the bar. No. About six inches further up-stage. There! And the other on top of it, with the fingers pointing the same way. (*To the* OTHERS.) I'm sure that's the way Mr. Robinson placed them.

MCAULIFFE

Well, that's the way they were when Briggs took 'em. Weren't they, Briggs?

BRIGGS

Yes.

MARIA (*hesitates, looks at* MCAULIFFE *intently for a moment, then continues*)

Never mind. We'll come back to it.

CLEVELAND

What's next?

BRIGGS (*reading*)

Lord Harry takes coin from pocket, throws it on the bar. "To pay for your broken crockery, landlord."

JESSUP

"There'll be naught broke, save your wishbone, maybe."

MARIA

Now you cross, Mr. Briggs. Over to Mr. Torrence. That's it. And you're further up-stage, Mr. Mc-Auliffe.

MCAULIFFE

Me? Up-stage?

MARIA

Yes. Much further.

MCAULIFFE

Never. I always played it down here.

MARIA

Not tonight, Mr. McAuliffe. You were much further up. Will you move, please?
[*He moves up a little.*

MCAULIFFE

I guess it don't matter, one way or the other.

MARIA

No. Further.

MCAULIFFE

I tell you—

MARIA (*sharply*)

*Further!*

MCAULIFFE (*scornfully, moving up a little further*)

Does this suit you?

MARIA

Yes, right there. Now, as regards the gloves themselves.—When we began just now, I noticed that one of the gloves had been turned the other way about, on the bar.

CLEVELAND

Of what importance is that?

LANE (*coming forward*)

I think I see Miss Scott's point. The glove might

account for the absence of finger-prints on the knife.

MARIA

Exactly! (*Turning to* JESSUP.) It's your speech, Mr. Jessup.

JESSUP (*nudging* CARLOTTA)

"Don't 'ee want to see him let the air into thy sweetheart?"

MRS. MONTGOMERY

"Leave the girl be!"
[*She slaps him lightly on the mouth. He moves, as before.* TORRENCE *and* BRIGGS *stand back to back.*

CLEVELAND

"Are you ready?"

MARIA

Your arm about her waist, Mr. Cleveland.

CLEVELAND (*complying*)

Yes, of course.

BRIGGS

You say, "Ready as rain," Clarke.

TORRENCE

Do I?

MARIA

Yes, but you didn't. And Mr. McAuliffe interpolated —"Are you ready, Jemmy?"

MCAULIFFE

"*Be* ye ready, Jemmy?" I said.

TORRENCE

I seem to have balled everything up. Did I say any-thing then?

MARIA

You said, "Aye, aye."

TORRENCE

Good for me! All right—"Aye, aye."

MARIA

Now, throw yourself, Miss Maxwell.

CARLOTTA (*throwing herself upon* TORRENCE)

"I beg thee—I beg thee!"

TORRENCE

"Get off, thou slut! Thou bag of—" What is that choice collection of words, again? Something about a leech?

BRIGGS (*reading*)

"Who'll pluck this leech off me?"

TORRENCE

That's it: "Who'll pluck this leech off me?"
[DR. GRACE *and* MRS. MONTGOMERY *drag* CARLOTTA *to the back of the room.*

BRIGGS

"Have no fear for me, my pretty chick."

CLEVELAND

"Are you—"

MARIA (*interrupting*)

One moment! (*To* CARLOTTA.) That was where you looked toward the door, Miss Maxwell.

CARLOTTA

Yes.

MARIA

And you saw Mr. Lane standing there?

CARLOTTA

I—

CLEVELAND

That's all been cleared up. Once more—"Are you ready?"

MARIA (*to* MCAULIFFE)

You're further up, Mr. McAuliffe.

MCAULIFFE (*moving up again*)

Whatever you say.

MARIA

That's right. Go on, Mr. Torrence.

TORRENCE

"Since yesterday, thick-skull!"

MARIA

Stop! (*To* CARLOTTA.) There's where you said—"Oh no, no, no!"

CARLOTTA

I don't remember, but I suppose you're right.

MARIA

Yes, I am!

LANE (*suddenly rushing forward*)

Wait a minute!

[*They all look at his in astonishment.*

CARLOTTA

What's the matter, Dickie?

LANE

I think I've—(*He stops.*) Oh, nothing—it's nothing at all. Please go on.

MARIA

Please continue, Mr. Briggs.

BRIGGS

"Give us—"

CARLOTTA

"Oh no—no—no!"

BRIGGS

"Give us the count."

CLEVELAND (*counting*)

"One—two—three—four—five—six!"

[TORRENCE *and* BRIGGS *advance one step at each count.*

MARIA

Now stop! And don't move, anyone, until I tell you. Now! Turn—aim—fire! (*Clapping her hands.*) Bang! Bang! Wait, please! And the off-stage guns at the same time—Bang—Bang! Bang—Bang! Then the jar broke, and you craned forward, Miss Maxwell, to see what had happened. Now drop the pistol, Mr. Briggs.

BRIGGS

Drop pistol. And then I say, "God! It caught me—!"

MRS. MAXWELL

No, no! He didn't say that!

CARLOTTA

Something about being shot.

MRS. MONTGOMERY

He said, "My God, I'm killed!"                    (together)

DR. GRACE

No, I don't think so. "A bullet!"
he said, or something like that.

CLEVELAND

It seemed just a cry of pain to me. There weren't
any words.

JESSUP

As I heard it, what he said was—

MARIA

Don't move anybody!

MCAULIFFE

Well, what did he say? (*Jeering.*) What a swell
bunch of witnesses! Some team-play, that is! All of
you right here within ten feet of him, and no two of
you heard him say the same thing!

DR. GRACE

We weren't expecting—

MCAULIFFE

You mean the murderer didn't send out a printed

program and a libretto, the way they usually do.

CLEVELAND

The exact words are not important. The point is—

MCAULIFFE (*interrupting him*)

No? Well, will you listen to the lawyer! Not important, eh? It's on the testimony of you people that somebody is going to be put on trial for this job— and you can't even agree about what a man said when he was shot. That's pretty damned important, it seems to me!

MARIA

What he said was—"Stop! Stop! I—" And then he put his hand to his chest like this. (*Illustrating.*) Let's go on, please—but very, very slowly. (*Darting forward.*) Mr. Briggs, you come straight forward to this spot. But very slowly. And the rest of you come slowly up to your positions. Like this—(*She indicates the pace.*) Just a moment. Now! (*She resumes her place.*) Now, when I count three, begin. Are you all ready? (*They nod silently.*) All right then. One—two—three! (*They all begin to move very slowly toward the spot she has indicated.*) Not so quickly, Mrs. Montgomery, if you please. That's better. Now if you don't mind, just wait there a second. I'm trying to recall—Mr. McAuliffe, it seems to me—did you, perhaps, lean forward at that point— accidentally displacing one of the gloves, perhaps?

MCAULIFFE

You ought to know. You were watching, weren't you?

MARIA

Yes, but naturally my attention was concentrated on Mr. Robinson and the group around him.

MCAULIFFE

I never moved once!

MARIA

I seem to remember your leaning forward, or some sudden movement as though you were startled.

MCAULIFFE

No. I never moved once—I was frozen stiff for a moment there.

MARIA (*moving to the front of the group*)

It was only with the corner of my eye that I saw you, but you did move. However, let's go on. All right, everybody, please. Ready, I'll count. Now—One—two—three! Now wait. You were much further up, Mr. McAuliffe—much further—and you were closer to Mr. Robinson, Mrs. Montgomery—almost touching him. And you, Mrs. Maxwell, you were right next to Mrs. Montgomery and just a little behind her. There! That's exactly the position. Now, from these positions, it's obvious—

LANE (*interrupting*)

I know what you're going to say! That Carlotta held that knife.

CARLOTTA (*quietly*)

I didn't, Dickie.

LANE

I know damned well you didn't.

MARIA

It couldn't have been anyone else. The dagger slashed Mrs. Montgomery's left sleeve, and from Miss Maxwell's position—

LANE

I don't care anything about that! Carlotta didn't do it!

MCAULIFFE

No? Then who did?

LANE

I'll tell you who I think it was, if you want to know— [*A series of sharp knocks begins to be heard at the outer door off Right.*

CARLOTTA (*screams*)

What's that?

CLEVELAND

The police!

CARLOTTA

Dickie, don't let them take me!

LANE

You bet I won't!

MCAULIFFE

Let 'em in, Maria.

MARIA (*starting to go*)

Yes sir.

LANE

Don't move, anybody!

MCAULIFFE (*starting for door*)

Look here, it's time—

LANE (*producing and pointing a revolver*)

I said, don't move! *This* was for Robinson, too. But someone else did a more thorough job of it—not Carlotta, though, nor any of the others around Robinson, either.

MCAULIFFE

Who did, then?

LANE

The man who turned that glove a few minutes ago! You! !

MCAULIFFE

What are you talking about?

LANE

You know damned well what I'm talking about! You gave us a false alarm, so you'd have a chance to turn that glove.

MCAULIFFE

Who says it was turned?

LANE

Miss Scott—the girl with the camera eye. She kodaks as she goes.

MARIA

What does that prove?

LANE

Prove? Why, Good God, it proves everything!

MCAULIFFE

Hear the boy rave, will you!

CLEVELAND

Wait a minute, Lane. You're a long way from proof.

LANE

I don't care. The man who touched that glove was the man who stabbed Robinson! And that was McAuliffe!

MCAULIFFE

Anybody can see, I wasn't within ten feet of him.

LANE

It doesn't matter. Somehow or other in the confusion of that scene, you stabbed him!

MARIA

McAuliffe was never anywhere near him.

MCAULIFFE

It's just a hang-over, Maria. (*To* LANE.) So that's your game, is it? You're going to frame this killing on me, are you?

LANE

I'm going to find out how you did it! (*The knocking of the police is heard again.*) Let them knock—they've waited this long, they can wait a bit longer. Now get back there, all of you. Where you were around Briggs! That's it! Now you, McAuliffe! Back where you were!

MCAULIFFE

Sure, anything you say. Going to pin the job on a

rank outsider, are you? Well, try and get away with it! Maybe I did it with a ten-foot spear—have you thought of that?

LANE

Bluff all you want. You did it with that knife that was in Robinson's back. And you used one of those gloves so there wouldn't be any finger-prints! That turned glove put me on the track. You're the only one that was close enough to it to have touched it without being seen! Step aside a minute!

MCAULIFFE

Say, I'm getting sick of this! Let the cops in!

LANE

Step aside, I say! And don't try any funny business! Hold your positions, all of you! Now you were up here in a corner, with everybody's attention on the duel scene. It would have been an easy matter for you to slip into one of those gloves without being seen.

MCAULIFFE

Yeah! And then to hit him on the head with an axe!

LANE

But how the hell did you manage to stab him?— By God, I've got it!

MARIA

What?

LANE

Don't move, please? From his position here, it was a straight line to Robinson's back—right between Carlotta and Mrs. Montgomery! You *threw* that knife, McAuliffe!

MCAULIFFE

Don't be a damn fool, Lane! Do you think you can convince anybody that a man would throw a knife into a crowd like that? Why nobody could make a shot like that!

LANE

An expert could! A trouper for thirty years, were you? What was your specialty? *A knife-throwing act!*

MCAULIFFE

Was it? I forget.

LANE

I guess it was, all right! I know what it is to be a crack shot. You get so you can't miss if you try— and you weren't trying to miss. You timed it just right, and threw to kill!

MCAULIFFE

Oh, I did, did I? Did you see me? Did anybody see me?

LANE

Maybe not. And I don't know why you did it, either. But I'm just as sure you did it, as if I had seen you! Why, the whole thing's as clear as day. You've rehearsed this thing for weeks! You picked the play— cast yourself for this part—and carefully arranged the positions so that there'd be five people around Robinson, on whom suspicion would naturally fall.

It was a damned good idea, McAuliffe, but you didn't figure on that turned glove, and that torn sleeve, and they gave you away!

MCAULIFFE

So, I'm caught, am I? Well, I guess not! Before you put the skids under me, you gotta take this case before a jury of plumbers, and real estate agents, and taxi-drivers, see? Just folks! I threw a knife, did I? Well where's your proof? Where's the man-jack that saw me do it? Ten of you right here on the stage, and six hundred of your friends out front—all the lights on—and you're going to tell a jury that I threw a knife! No two of you can remember what a man said, where he was shot, or whether somebody forgot a line or not. And you're going to try to sell twelve husky citizens the idea that I killed a bird!

LANE

Yes, I know—you counted on just that, too, didn't you?—Thought you had yourself nicely covered, but I guess circumstances are a little too incriminating!

MCAULIFFE

Listen, Lane: I've got no hard feelings against you for this. I know how a kid feels when he's in love with a girl. He—

MRS. MONTGOMERY (*suddenly*)

Miss Clinton!

LANE

What?

MRS. MONTGOMERY

Mary Clinton!

LANE

Who's she? What about her?— Oh—

CARLOTTA

That letter—it was from a girl named Mary Clinton.
[LANE *again turns on* MCAULIFFE.

LANE

—That slip of your tongue awhile ago—Who's
Mary Clinton—and what do you know about her and
Robinson?

MRS. MONTGOMERY

She was—she was—
[*She cannot go on.*

MRS. MAXWELL

—Wasn't she his assistant?

LANE

So she was!

MCAULIFFE

Well, what of it?

LANE

And maybe you were in love with her too, and Robinson took her! I guess that just about sews it up,
McAuliffe!

MARIA

What proof have you?

LANE

We'll soon get the proof! All we have to do, is get
hold of this Clinton girl, and get the whole story
from her!

MCAULIFFE

You can save yourself the trouble. She died three days ago.
[*There is a silence. The knocking of the police is again heard.*

CLEVELAND

Let the police in, Hal.
[BRIGGS *goes out.*

LANE (*impulsively*)

You had damned good cause to kill him, McAuliffe, and I hope to God they don't convict you!

MCAULIFFE

Thanks Lane, they won't. They won't convict anyone.

CLEVELAND

But with Miss Scott's testimony —

MARIA (*interrupting quickly*)

—*My* testimony? *I* didn't see a thing! How could I, with *my* eyes?
[*She takes off her glasses and begins to polish them, blinking rapidly.* MCAULIFFE *smiles confidently.*

MCAULIFFE

Good girl, Maria. You were all that worried me. (*He calls off Left.*) Right this way, Officers!
[*He covers his mouth with his hand and stands waiting for them, laughing silently to himself.*

CURTAIN